SECOND CHANCE

CREDIT
RESTORATION BOOK

Even though Life Line Credit Corporation has done its best to make sure that all the information in this book is as accurate as possible, still, in this rapidly-changing industry, mergers, acquisitions, relocation of companies occur frequently and interest rates may change daily. Therefore, we cannot guarantee the accuracy of any information at the time of use by the consumer.

In no event will Life Line Credit Corporation be liable for direct, indirect, identical, or consequential damages resulting from any information in this book, or damages for loss of business profits, business interruption, or other monetary losses, even if the consumer has been advised of the possibility of such damages.

Company names appearing in this book are registered trademarks of their respective companies.

If you have any comments or ideas regarding *Second Chance*, or to order additional copies, please contact

Final Touch Corp c/o Life Line Credit
6609 Riesterstown Rd.
Baltimore MD 21215
Phone:410-358 4499   Fax.: 410-358 4685
E-mail: ftouch@aol.com

ACKNOWLEDGMENT

I would like to express my heartfelt thanks to the people who assisted me in the production of this book: Mr. David Evgey and Ms. Betty Cherniak, co-authors, Ms. Toby Stein, editor and Mr. Derrick Harris, graphic design. Without their dedication, hard work, expertise and creativity, this endeavor could never have come to fruition.

Iraj M. Forutan

TABLE OF CONTENTS

<u>SECTION 4</u>   APPENDICES

INTRODUCTION

Credit is essential for anyone today. Without a credit card, you will have trouble renting a car or reserving a hotel room. Trying to buy something on the telephone from a direct marketer without a credit card presents definite problems. For instance, paying by check wastes time two ways: first, for the check to arrive and then for it to clear. Carrying large amounts of cash when you travel can be hazardous. If your expenses are business-related or otherwise reimbursable, credit card receipts are often vital back-up.

The good news is that, even if you have had credit problems in the past, you can repair your credit rating without hiring someone to do it for you. Credit restoration companies charge for their services, often lavishly, and may indulge in practices which are not necessarily legal. Their advice may even cause you innocently to take steps that are against the law.

The do-it-yourself methods described in this book put the solution to credit problems in your own hands.

This book is divided into four sections:

Section One tells you how to restore your credit by repairing your credit report on your own. The credit report is the single most important tool your creditors use to decide whether to grant you credit and, if so, how much to give you. This section shows you how to obtain, understand, and, when necessary, rectify your credit report - the only sure-fire way to rehabilitate your credit rating.

What if your credit record is good? The fact is, you can't be sure it *is* good unless you know what's in your credit report. If your report contains errors, these can hurt you when you apply for credit in the future. A recent government study has shown that more than 40% of all credit reports contain errors, so it is essential to know what yours contains.

Whatever your credit history, following the advice in this section will enable you to be confident that your credit rating is in good order.

Section Two shows you how to establish a sound credit record from scratch. It also tells you everything you need to know to be able to increase your credit and maintain that good credit rating.

This part of the book also deals in helpful detail with the basic credit tool, credit cards. Section Two discusses the different types of cards, how to calculate the cost of credit, and how to evaluate the wide range of options available.

Whenever you use a credit card, you are taking out a loan at a very high interest rate. *Second Chance* will show you how to use credit cards wisely and keep your credit costs to a minimum.

Section Three includes the full texts of laws that impact on credit and credit repair. Preceding each text, we have included a summary describing the key points of each law in order to enable you to exercise your full rights as a consumer.

Section Four contains extensive information about credit card companies and the rates they offer, as well as other useful information about each card.

We have also included addresses which will help you manage and repair your use of credit, and a glossary that defines key terms used in the world of credit.

Finally, at the end of Section Four you will find a brief history of credit, which traces how we became a country of borrowers - in need of a book like *Second Chance*.

The process of repairing credit is neither short nor easy, but if you consistently follow the guidelines provided in *Second Chance*, you will be able to achieve your goal: a good credit report. And if you maintain that new credit rating in the ways we suggest, you will in future qualify for all the credit you need.

The information in this book is accurate and up-to-date. However, in the rapidly changing credit industry, company names, telephone numbers and, most importantly, interest rates change frequently. We recommend that, when you contact any of the listed companies or organizations, you verify such details.

We welcome your comments and suggestions and would like to hear your ideas. Please don't hesitate to contact us.

SECTION ONE

HOW TO RESTORE YOUR CREDIT

RATING ON YOUR OWN

CHAPTER 1

WHAT YOU NEED TO KNOW ABOUT CREDIT BUREAUS

The Big Three

There are three major nationwide credit bureaus. Each bureau provides detailed consumer credit information to creditors, employers and insurance companies. TRW, Equifax, and Trans Union have over 220 million consumer names in their databases.

- TRW Consumer Information Service is one of the nation's largest credit bureaus. TRW provides a number of credit reporting services and was one of the first credit bureaus to use artificial intelligence to access consumer credit reports through a database.

- Trans Union Consumer Information Co. has been providing credit reporting services since 1988. Trans Union developed one of the first on-line credit retrieval computer systems in the United States. Credit Reporting On-Line Network Utility Retrieval Data Processing System, or CRONUS, provides nationwide service to creditors and other businesses. With its fast and accurate reporting capabilities, CRONUS can provide consumer credit reports in just seconds.

- Equifax Credit Information Service was established to provide creditors in Atlanta access to consumer credit histories. Today, Equifax not only offers its services throughout the U.S., it also provides consumer credit history services to Canada. In 1987, Equifax and CSC Credit Services merged their databases and now support 1,100 locations in the United States, Canada, and Europe.

What Services Do the Bureaus Provide?

- They store and receive consumers' credit histories

- They assist creditors in direct marketing by providing mailing lists of potential consumers who meet each creditor's criteria for credit campaigns.

Other services include: insurance underwriting, collection of accounts, and research on the latest technology to improve systems operations.

What Information Gets Reported?

The Fair Credit Reporting Act was passed to protect consumers by ensuring that credit bureaus were reporting factual information. It also gives the consumer legal recourse if a credit bureau refuses to abide by the law. See Chapter 17 for the summary and complete text of the FCRA.

What FCRA Says About How Information is Accumulated:

- The information found in a credit report is obtained from creditors and financial institutions, public records, businesses and any other source in which a consumer has created a debt or bill. The consumer also contributes to the information that is placed on the credit report.

- Every time a consumer fills out a credit application, the information from that application is placed or updated on the credit report.

What If the Information Isn't Correct?

- The credit bureau has a legal obligation to report accurate and factual information. If it is brought to the attention of a credit bureau that their files contain erroneous information, it is the responsibility of the credit bureau to investigate that charge and, if it holds up, correct the information.

- Consumers have the right to obtain a copy of their credit report, dispute inaccurate information, and have a brief summary of their side of any unresolved dispute placed in the credit report.

Figure 1-1 shows how credit bureaus obtain the information for credit reports.

Figure 1-1

Credit Bureaus receive consumer
information from several resources..

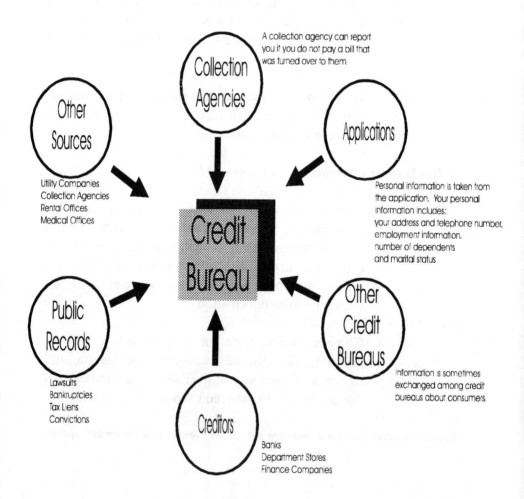

Collection Agencies

A collection agency can report
you if you do not pay a bill that
was turned over to them.

Other Sources

Utility Companies
Collection Agencies
Rental Offices
Medical Offices

Applications

Personal information is taken from
the application. Your personal
information includes:
your address and telephone number,
employment information,
number of dependents
and marital status

Credit Bureau

Public Records

Lawsuits
Bankruptcies
Tax Liens
Convictions

Other Credit Bureaus

Information is sometimes
exchanged among credit
bureaus about consumers.

Creditors

Banks
Department Stores
Finance Companies

Example:

Kenneth Chandon fills out an application for credit. This is the first time he's applied for credit. All the information he divulges on the credit application will be placed in his credit report, including: his home address, phone number, date of birth, Social Security number, marital status, employment, and salary. If Kenneth already has a credit report, any new information provided by him on the application will be used to up-date his credit report.

The FCRA also governs who can look at your credit report. There are certain restrictions on the procedures followed by credit bureaus for divulging credit information to persons who request a report.

- A creditor, an insurance company, or a potential employer may look at your credit report. However, each of them must have substantial proof of identification before the credit bureau shows them your credit report.

- Any business requesting a copy of a credit report must demonstrate a legitimate business need for seeing that report.

Overview of How the Big Three Work

The main objective of each credit bureau is to collect and report information to credit grantors.

Credit grantors that lend and extend credit include:

- banks

- department stores
- mortgage companies
- other financial institutions which lend money

Credit bureaus receive revenue on each report issued to credit lenders, insurance companies, potential employers, and consumers. The cost for a credit report ranges from $2.00 to $40.00. Computer systems make it possible for your credit report to be obtained almost anywhere in the United States.

Automatic and Associated Subscribers also have access to your credit report.

- Automatic Subscribers - for example, banks and department stores - supply credit bureaus with payment histories on a regular basis. A computer tape is provided to the credit bureau each month and the credit histories are updated. Automatic subscribers like banks and department stores are charged a monthly fee, according to the terms of their particular membership agreement with the credit bureau.

- Associated Subscribers - utility companies, landlords and insurance companies are among those who fall into this category - have agreements with the Big Three through which they have access to credit reports.

The following entities might request your credit report:

- A landlord looks at a potential renter's credit report

to see if he would be a good candidate to rent an apartment.

- The local utility company looks at a credit report to see if a consumer pays bills on time.

Additional businesses that might need to look at your credit report include:

- telephone companies
- credit unions
- hospitals
- insurance companies

Although credit bureaus exist mainly to serve the purposes of credit grantors, as a credit consumer you have a vested interest in the reliability of their reports. *What they say about you matters.*

> **If you do not use any credit for seven years, your credit report will be eliminated. If you have filed bankruptcy, this will stay on your credit report for 10 years.**

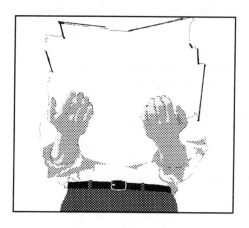

CHAPTER 2

HOW TO FIND OUT WHAT CREDIT BUREAUS KNOW ABOUT YOU

How to Locate a National or Local Credit Bureau

You learned about the Big Three credit bureaus in Chapter One. TRW, Equifax, and Trans Union provide credit reports and credit information to approximately 250 "Super Bureaus" nationwide. These "Super Bureaus" usually purchase credit reports in bulk and then resell them to smaller credit agencies, the automatic and associated reporting bureaus we mentioned on page 5.

Automatic reporting bureaus are computer-automated and are affiliated with or owned by one of the Big Three. Smaller reporting agencies, on the other hand, usually track consumers' payment records in a locality.

The smaller credit bureaus obtain their information directly from the Big Three. To check on your credit rating, it might be easier, quicker

and cheaper to call a local bureau than to go directly to one of the
Big Three. It's probably worth your time to call a few local agencies,
compare what they charge for a report, and find out how long each
would take to get your credit report and pass it on to you.

You can locate a local credit reporting agency by using the Yellow
Pages (look under "credit" or "credit rating and reporting") or by
calling information (411).

If you decide instead to go with the Big Three, ask your potential
creditor which bureau the company uses and contact that one. This
will guarantee that you are dealing with the same credit report as
your creditor. As a general principle, however, it is strongly
recommended that, *before you have an immediate reason*, you obtain
a copy of your credit report from each of the Big Three. These
bureaus do not exchange information among themselves; therefore,
the credit history each has on you may contain different information.
It's in your self-interest to know what all of them say.

Obtaining a Copy of Your Credit Report

In most cases, you can call the credit reporting agency and request
a copy of your credit report via a voice mail message. If you are
directed to submit a written request, you will receive instructions
over the voice mail service.

The credit bureau will usually send out a credit report within 72
hours of receiving a voice mail message. However, there is no
guarantee that your voice mail message will be received. Nor will
there be a written record of such a message. Therefore, even though
voice mail service is available, requesting your credit report in writing

is a more reliable option. Or, if you do leave a voice mail message, be sure to follow it up with a written request. Usually you will have to pay a small fee for the report.

How to Contact the Big Three

For your convenience, in the figures that follow we provide you with the telephone numbers and addresses of the Big Three. You will also find the fees for additional reports and payment information.

TRW will provide you with one free report per year, and a free report if you have been denied credit within the past 30 days. Equifax and Trans Union charge $8.00 per report (in most states), and will issue a free report if you have been denied credit within the past 60 days.

Credit Bureau	Address and Phone #	Fees	After Being Denied Credit
TRW	TRW Consumer Information Service P.O. Box 1009 Allen, TX 75002-1009 Phone: 800-392-1122 English and Spanish 24 hour voice mail system	First report free. For additional reports, the fee is $8.00. If you live in Maine, the report is $2.00 and in Maryland, $5.00.	One free report if credit has been denied within the past 30 days.

Credit Bureau	Address and Phone #	Fees	After Being Denied Credit
Equifax	Equifax Information Service Center P.O. Box 105873 Atlanta, GA 30348 Phone: 800-685-1111 24-hour voice mail system Fax 404-612-2668	Reports are $8.00. First report free for consumers living in Maryland, and each additional report is $5.00. First report free for consumers living in Vermont, each additional report is $7.50. Reports are $3.00 in Maine.	One free report if credit has been denied within the past 60 days.
Trans Union	Trans Union Consumer Information Service P.O. Box 390 Springfield, PA 19064-0390 Phone: 216-779-7200 24 hour voice-mail system	Reports are mailed within 72 hours. Reports are $8.00 for an individual and $16.00 for a joint report for you and your spouse.	One report free if credit has been denied within the past 60 days.

How to Get a Copy of Your Credit Report in Writing

If you request a copy of your credit report in writing, TRW, Equifax and Trans Union will ask you to provide the following information:

- First, middle and last name

- Seniority terms (e.g., Sr., Jr., II, III)

- Current address (street address, city, state and zip code)

- If you moved within the past five years, you will need to list a previous address (street address, city, state, and zip code)

- Daytime and evening telephone numbers

- Social Security number

- Date of birth

- If you are married, you will need to include your spouse's name, his or her Social Security number, and date of birth.

- Written proof of your current address (e.g. a *copy* of your utility bill, valid driver's license, or major credit card statement).

- **VERY IMPORTANT**: Sign your request letter.

Figure 2-1 is a sample request letter for a credit report.

If you incorporate all this information in your letter, most credit bureaus will send out your credit report within five days after receiving your request.

Obtaining a Copy of Your Credit Report When Denied Credit

If you have been denied credit, and would like to receive a free copy of your credit report, you must request the report in a timely way:

- For TRW - within 30 days of receiving your denial letter.

- For Equifax and Trans Union - within 60 days of the denial letter's arrival.

If the creditor who denied you credit used a credit reporting agency other than the Big Three, the location of the agency will probably be noted in the denial letter. If this information is missing, you may be able to locate the credit reporting agency through the Yellow Pages, or you may call the creditor directly and ask him for the name and address of the credit bureau that provided him with a copy of your credit report.

Please note: In addition to the information outlined on page 11, your request should include a copy of the denial letter from the creditor who denied you credit.

Figure 2-1

To Request A Credit Report

Your Name
Address
Phone Number
Social Security Number
Date
Address of Credit Bureau

Re: Credit Report

Dear Sir or Madam:
I have enclosed a check (check number and amount) to have a
copy of my credit report sent to me. I have enclosed the
required information for proof of identification and adddress.
First, middle and last name (including: Seniority Terms[e.g., Sr.,
Jr., II]
Current address (street address, city, state and zip code).
Previous address (if you moved within the past five years-street
address,city, state, and zip code).
Daytime telephone number   Evening telephone number
Social Security number   Date of Birth (e.g.,June 12, 1967)

If you are married: Your spouse's name, Social Security number
and date of birth.

Written proof of my current address is enclosed(copy of utility
bill, valid driver's license, major credit card statement).

Please send my credit report as soon as posible. Thank you.
Sincerely,

John Smith

John Smith

**The Top 15 Credit Card Issuers Ranked by Number of
Cardholder Accounts***

1. Discover Card	29,500,000
2. Citicorp	20,000,000
3. AT&T Universal Card	12,000,000
4. First Chicago Corp.	11,000,000
5. Household Credit Services	10,500,000
6. MBNA America	8,500,000
7. Chase Manhattan Corp.	8,000,000
8. BankAmerica	7,000,000
9. Banc One Corp.	6,500,000
10. American Express Centurion	5,300,000
11. Chemical Bank Retail Card Services	5,250,000
12. Bank of New York	4,800,000
13. Associates National Bank	4,700,000
14. NationsBank of Delaware	4,100,000
15. First USA Bank	4,000,000

* All figures are estimates

**Figure 2-2 shows a sample request letter for a credit report when you have
been denied credit.**

Now that you know how to obtain your credit report, the next step
is understanding it. Chapter Three is designed to help you do that.

Figure 2-2

To Request A Credit Report When You Have Been Denied

Your Name
Address
Phone Number
Social Security Number
Date
Address of Credit Bureau

Re: Credit Report

Dear Sir or Madam:

I have enclosed a check (check number and amount) to have a copy of my credit report sent to me. I have enclosed the required information for proof of identification and adddress.
First, middle and last name (including: Seniority Terms[e.g., Sr., Jr., II]
Current address (street address, city, state and zip code).
Previous address (if you moved within the past five years-street address,
city, state, and zip code).
Daytime telephone number   Evening telephone number
Social Security number   Date of Birth (e.g.,June 12, 1967)

If you are married: Your spouse's name, Social Security number and date of birth.

Written proof of my current address is enclosed(copy of utility bill, valid driver's license, major credit card statement).

Also enclosed is a photocopy of the letter denying me credit. Please send my credit report as soon as posible. Thank you.

Sincerely,

John Smith

John Smith

CHAPTER 3

MAKING SENSE OF YOUR CREDIT REPORT

When Do You Need to Know What's in Your Credit Report?

Look at what happened to Ed Masterson - and then decide.

Ed was a successful family man. He had a good job with a better-than-decent income and excellent benefits, a wife, and two children.

Then, when he least expected it, his company was bought out by a larger firm. Ed was one of the victims of the down-sizing that followed almost immediately.

After he lost his job, despite his best efforts, he couldn't keep up with his usual bills. His payments were late more than once.

Ed looked hard for a job like the one he lost. When he had no luck, he began to look for a job at a lower salary. This search, too, was unsuccessful. Eventually, out of desperation, Ed decided to go into business for himself. After all, he still had his skills and lots of experience.

He applied for a small business loan at his local bank and his loan application was rejected. The reason: negative entries on his credit report.

When Ed got a copy of the credit report, he found that the negative entries were not in line with the facts. What was stopping him from getting a loan were errors in his report!

Ed Masterson was able to repair his credit report, but the process took months of precious time which should have been used in opening and running his business. As a result, his financial situation got worse and worse.

If Ed had gotten a copy of his credit report *before he needed it*, he could have corrected the problems then and saved himself a lot of grief and wasted time.

Don't wait until *your* entire future may depend on your ability to obtain credit. Find out now what's in your credit report. In most cases, mistakes in your report can be corrected and negative items deleted. So get your report and check it out carefully. If there are mistakes, set about having them corrected - as soon as possible. That way, you won't end up like Ed Masterson!

What Goes on a Credit Report?

Your credit report presents a profile of your credit history.

When credit reports were first used, almost anything could be reported. Credit investigators were rewarded for obtaining negative information about people, whether founded or unfounded. The credit investigator would interview the consumer's neighbors and if the neighbors had negative information, the investigator would promptly place this information in the credit report. All the investigator had to do was take the neighbor's name so that his supervisor had a starting point to verify the validity of the statement. Sometimes, however, there was no follow-up by a supervisor. As a result, some people were denied credit simply because creditors would read what a neighbor mistakenly *thought* was true.

With the passage of the Equal Credit Opportunity Act in 1975, the granting of credit could no longer be based on the whim of the creditor or hearsay from a neighbor. Consumers now have specific rights and, if they need to defend those rights, have legal recourse available.

Figure 3-1 shows a typical credit report.

Information on the credit report falls into two broad categories: personal and public.

Sample Report

Figure 3-1

NAME AND ADDRESS OF CREDIT BUREAU MAKING REPORT

	SINGLE REFERENCE		IN FILE REPORT		TRADE REPORT
Sample Consumer Credit Report	[X] FULL REPORT		EMPLOY & TRADE REPORT		PREVIOUS RESIDENCE REPORT
123 Charge Rd., Ste. 4500					
Limit, NY, 12345		OTHER			

		DATE RECEIVED 2-4-91	CONFIDENTIAL
FOR	Department Store X	DATE MAILED 2-1-91	
	345 Charlie Ave.	IN FILE SINCE 10-7-79	■ MEMBER ASSOCIATED CREDIT BUREAU, INC.
	Down, DE 00012	INQUIRED AS:	

REPORT ON: LAST NAME	FIRST NAME	INITIAL	SOCIAL SECURITY NUMBER	SPOUSE'S NAME
Consumer	Charlie	N.	789-78-7890	Patricia Marie

ADDRESS:	CITY	STATE	ZIP CODE	SINCE:	SPOUSE'S SOCIAL SECRUTIY NO.
15 1st St.	Drew	DE	00015	1986	123-45-6789

PRESENT EMPLOYER:	POSITION HELD:	SINCE:	DATE EMPLOY VERIFIED	EST. MONTHLY INCOME
Big Company Inc.	Plant Mgr.	1982	1985	3,600 $

DATE OF BIRTH	NUMBER OF DEPENDENTS INCLUDING SELF: 4	[X] OWNS OR BUYING HOME	RENTS HOME	OTHER: (EXPLAIN)
1-11-62				

FORMER ADDRESS:	CITY:		STATE:	FROM:	TO
31 Herbert St., Apt. 3D	Drew	DE	1980	1986	

FORMER EMPLOYER:	POSITION HELD:	FROM:	TO:		EST. MONTHLY INCOME
The Small Group	Purchasing Agent	1979	1982		3,000 $

SPOUSE'S EMPLOYER:	POSITION HELD:	SINCE:	DATE EMPLOY VERIFIED	EST. MONTHLY INCOME
Lincoln Elementary School	Teacher	1985	1986	2,400 $

WHOSE	KIND OF BUSINESS AND ID CODE	DATE REPORTED AND METHOD OF REPORTING	DATE OPENED	DATE OF LAST PAYMENT	HIGHEST CREDIT OR LAST CONTRACT	PRESENT STATUS		PAST DUE		HISTORICAL STATUS			TYPE & TERMS (MANNER OF PAYMENT)	REMARKS
						BALANCE OWING	AMOUNT	NO. OF PAY(IE.M)	30 I.M MO PLY REPAYREF	30-60 DAYS ONLY	60-90 DAYS ONLY	90 E.MO AND OVER		
I	DEP-D776	01-30-91	05-12-79	01-15-91	2,000	500	50	34	48	1	2	0	Rev.	
J	BAN-B442	01-30-91	11-15-80	01-16-91	1,000	200	0	14	24	0	0	0	Open	
A	BAN-B567	01-30-91	02-07-90	12-01-89	500	0	0	0	0	0	0	0	Rev.	
I	BAN-B789	01-30-91	04-13-89	01-16-91	3,500	1,500	0	18	20	0	0	0	Rev.	

Judgement Filed 10-19-87, Gothem District Court, Case Number - 56789-09
Defendant - Charlie Consumer, Amount $500; Plaintiff - Red Wood Co.; Satisfied 11/87.
Verified 6/88.

*************************Companies That Requested Your Credit History***********************

09-07-90	Bank America
06-12-87	Sears
03-17-82	Bank of Delaware
07-15-81	PM Citibank

Personal Information

Personal information includes your:

- full name
- current and previous address
- telephone number
- date and place of birth
- Social Security number
- marital status
- current and previous employment information
- whether you rent or own your home.

If you are married, the report will list your married name as well. From a creditor's point of view, home ownership is preferable to renting and being married is preferable to being single.

Example:

Jane Smith marries John Doe; they decide to combine names. On the report Jane's married name will be Jane Doe-Smith and John's name will be John Doe-Smith.

If you use nicknames, like Jim for James, the report will list not only James but also Jim. If you use an alias to obtain credit, the alias will also appear on the credit report. (It is not advisable to use an alias.)

In addition to your name, address, and phone number, your employment history will be on the credit report. Your employment history includes both present and former positions, listing:

- the company name
- your position with the company
- dates of employment
- your salary

If you are married, your spouse's employment history will also be on the credit report.

There have been occasions where an individual's credit information has been recorded on the credit report of another family member - one of many good reasons to check your credit report once a year.

You cannot be sure what is being reported unless you see the report. So be on the safe side - take the initiative and find out exactly what is on your credit report.

Public Information

Public information includes anything resulting from legal action taken by you or against you, such as:

- lawsuits
- tax liens
- court judgments
- bankruptcies

Any court judgment pertaining to money will be reported on your credit report.

Example:

Jim Smith sues Doug Brown for an unpaid debt of $500. The judge
rules for the plaintiff, Jim Smith, and orders Doug Brown to pay $500.
This judgment will be placed on Doug's credit report, *whether or not
he pays the debt.*

Example of a court judgment on a credit report:

June County Small Claims Court Case #12-ABC345, 2/95
Plaintiff Jim Smith $500   Paid 1/3/95

        Or:

June County Small Claims Court Case #12-ABC345, 2/95
Plaintiff Jim Smith $500   Not Paid

Any court order such as garnishment of wages or frozen bank
accounts will also be listed on your credit report. Bankruptcies are
reported on your credit report for 10 years.

Inquiries

Every time someone requests a copy of your credit report, the inquiry
itself becomes an added item. For example, if you apply for a credit
card with Sears, the request will appear on your credit report,
regardless of whether or not your application is approved. For this
reason, it is better not to apply too often for any kind of credit,
whether credit cards or charge accounts; this could indicate to a
potential creditor that you might be overextending yourself financially.

Charge Accounts and Loans

All individual and joint charge accounts and loans will appear on your credit report. Mortgages will also be reported.

Debts to Local Businesses

Records of payments to the following are reported only if you are delinquent on the payments:

- doctors
- dentists
- landlords
- lawyers
- private investigators
- insurance companies
- utility companies
- telephone companies
- specialty stores

Example:

Nancy McAdams switched car insurance companies and did not make the last payment on her original insurance policy. The first insurance company not only sent her account to the company's collections department, but also reported her debt to the credit bureau.

What <u>Could</u> Be in Your Credit Report?

According to a recent government study, only 20% of all American consumers have seen their credit report, yet 40% of all credit reports contain incorrect and outdated information. This means that a lot of people have faulty credit reports. You need to make sure you're not one of them!

All the information in your report is taken very seriously by creditors. There have been many situations where people who have paid their bills in a timely way are turned down for credit because of misinformation in their credit report.

As a consumer, you need to be aware that your credit report may contain:

- Erroneous information
- Outdated information
- Irrelevant information
- Blemishes due to late payments
- Negative information, including accounts of old difficulties

Erroneous Information

Someone else's credit account could be listed on your credit report; or your credit account could be reported as having been closed when it is actually open.

Example:

Henry Nelson, a senior citizen with an excellent credit history, picked out a new car. Imagine his distress when he was refused financing because his credit report showed a number of late credit card payments - and even a few non-payments. Mr. Nelson's new car purchase was delayed several months while he grappled with the credit union which had issued the faulty report.

In the end, the problem was corrected - his credit report had gotten mixed up with that of someone with a similar name. (Mixed files are unfortunately not an unusual occurrence.) However, if Mr. Nelson had gotten a copy of his credit report before he needed it, the erroneous information would have been corrected before he applied for the car loan.

Outdated Information

It is not uncommon for someone to have a credit report which contains outdated information. This information can harm your credit rating by reflecting unfavorably on the stability of your living or working patterns. If the information you give to a potential creditor or landlord differs from that on your credit report, it can make you look dishonest or unreliable.

Outdated information includes:

- old addresses
- listings of negative information that are more than seven years old
- any other information that has changed.

Examples:

Sam has been working at a $70,000 per year job and owned his own home for five years, but his credit report states that his salary is $35,000 and he rents an apartment.

Felice's credit report listed her as single even though she has been married for four years.

Bob White moved from 2 First Street, New York, N.Y. to 34 Red
Avenue, Burlington, VT. When Bob asked for and received a copy
of his credit report two years later, the report still listed his New York
address.

Blemishes Due to Late Payments

Possibly the most damaging situation arises when an unfavorable
credit history continues to be held against you even though you
mended your ways several years ago and have been paying your bills
conscientiously ever since. The blemishes marring your credit record
are not a fair reflection of the consumer you are today, but so long as
they remain in place, they can deter potential creditors from granting
you credit.

Example:

Karen Elkenberg had credit problems when she was first starting out
in her career. On several occasions, she was delinquent on her credit
card and department store charge card payments. But in the past few
years, her position and income improved, and her payment patterns
were much better. She had almost forgotten about those hard times.

Unfortunately, the credit reporting agency hadn't forgotten. When
Karen wanted to buy a condominium, the bank officer told her that he
couldn't go ahead with the loan process. Karen found out that her
credit report listed several delinquencies which had never been cleared
up.

What were Karen's options at this point? She could wait for the seven-
year limit on negative entries, at which point this information would

automatically be removed from her credit report, or she could try to negotiate with her old creditors. Karen chose the latter option, contacted her old creditors, negotiated repayment in reasonable installments, and got them to agree to request removal of the information.

Only after this process was satisfactorily completed was she able to proceed with her home purchase. Clearly, it would have been to Karen's advantage to know her credit rating earlier and clear up the situation in a timely way.

Irrelevant Information

Sometimes credit reports contain information that has nothing whatsoever to do with your reliability as a consumer. Yet these entries can loom as stop signals to a potential creditor.

Example:

Michael dated a woman for two years. Even though he did not live at her address, nor have his mail delivered there, the woman's address was somehow recorded on Michael's credit report. The misinformation made it look as though Michael was not giving his correct address.

Negative Information

Negative information is any information that reflects poor credit habits, such as late payments or default of a credit account or loan.

By law, if such information cannot be verified, it must be removed. However, if you have had financial difficulties and the information is proven to be correct, you will have to wait seven years for it to be removed. Even in this situation, however, you still have the option of adding a consumer statement to your credit report explaining how and why you ended up with this mark against your credit. These statements are read by potential creditors and taken into consideration when granting you credit.

Too many of these statements, however, alert the creditor that you may not be serious enough about taking responsibility for your debts; therefore, you should use this privilege judiciously. (The most serious problem in this category is past bankruptcy, which calls for a ten-year removal wait. For more information on bankruptcy, see Chapter 6, page 53)

Example:

Keith Yardley knew when he filed for bankruptcy that this was a serious step, yet all he could think about was getting some much-needed relief from his terrible financial problems.

Four years later, his dire money situation seemed like a bad dream. Keith had gotten his financial affairs in order, and was ready to get on with his life. But whenever he tried to take a major step financially - buy a house or car - he was turned down flat. Why? Because the four-year-old bankruptcy was still on his credit report. It would be another six years until the ten-year bankruptcy limit would be reached and the bankruptcy would be deleted from Keith's credit report.

If **your** report contains any items similar to the examples given above, you are not being fairly represented by your credit report. What's more important, their presence may hinder you in obtaining credit.

That's why it is crucial that you know what your credit report says
about you.

Is the credit report in English - or in code?

Upon receiving your credit report, by law you must be provided with
a legend or key defining what each code means. Credit bureaus assign
coded letters or acronyms to your accounts to identify the type of
payment and payment history.

On your credit report, each account has a specific code. All
department store credit accounts are identified with the letter "D";
bank loans are identified with the letter "B"; and so on.

Example:

If you had a charge account with a jewelry store, the "K" in the key of
codes provided by the credit bureau would identify your account as a
jewelry store charge account. Another code would identify the
account's payment method (i.e., revolving, etc.). The credit bureau
would put the letter "K" next to your account number.

What you've got in writing now is the first part of your credit case
history. This will clarify in your own mind what the problems are. The
next step is to deal with them. In the next chapter, *Second Chance* will
show you how.

Remember, what you do from now on will determine the accuracy of
your credit report.

You have it in your power to create a debt-free credit record!

CHAPTER 4

WHAT TO DO ABOUT MISTAKES IN YOUR CREDIT REPORT

What You Need To Be On the Lookout For

The most common problem to be found in credit reports is erroneous information. As you saw in the last chapter, incorrect information can range from outdated addresses, telephone numbers, and names to blatantly incorrect statements that have nothing whatsoever to do with the person whose name is on the credit report.

The burden of catching errors in your credit report and seeing that they are corrected lies with you, the consumer. The responsibility of the credit bureau is to rectify an error you have discovered in your credit report, but only after you have contacted them with the correct information. That's why it's so important to obtain a credit report on a regular basis, check it and, when errors are found, begin the correction process.

Lawsuits have been filed against some of the Big Three: for combining credit reports from different people; and for failing to correct mistakes even after they have been brought to the attention of the credit bureau.

But a lawsuit is plainly a last resort. In most cases, misinformation will be corrected or deleted if you provide the credit bureau with what they need in order to make your report conform with the facts.

Correcting Errors on Your Credit Report

The process of correcting erroneous information is somewhat time-consuming, and requires a combination of patience and persistence.

The first step is to write to the credit bureau requesting an investigation into the information on the credit report you are questioning. Dispute only three items per letter. After your letter is sent, you will need to wait about 30 days for a response. If you do not receive a response, send a second letter to the credit bureau, citing your previous letter. If this still does not get you the corrections you need, send a third letter to the credit bureau, with a copy to the Federal Trade Commission. This is usually effective in alerting the credit bureau that you mean business, you know your legal rights, and you are not going to give up.

> **Check your credit report for positive information from creditors that may not appear. You have the right to have this information included on your credit report upon request.**

Figure 4-1 is a sample letter asking the credit bureau to have incorrect information removed from your credit report.

Figure 4-2 is a sample letter asking the credit bureau to have outdated information removed from your credit report.

Figure 4-3 shows a sample letter asking the credit bureau to reinvestigate incorrect information.

Each letter you send should go by certified mail/return receipt requested. The receipt will be proof that your letter was received.

If, after the above process has been completed, negative entries remain in your credit report, your next step will depend upon your particular situation and the nature of the negative entries.

At this point, you will have three main options:

1. Contact directly the creditors who asked for the negative entries to be placed in your credit report and negotiate with them to have these entries removed. If you still owe a creditor money, you might be able to work out a deal: in exchange for full payment or a schedule of installment payments, they may agree to allow the entries to be removed.

2. Place a consumer statement on your credit report explaining how and why you have marks against your credit. The consumer statement has to be 100 words or less, and you should not use this option carelessly - too many statements make you look like a poor credit risk. These statements are read and do help creditors understand that certain entries may have resulted from one-time difficulties and do not reflect upon you as an unreliable person.

Figure 4-1

Sample letter to the credit bureau to have incorrect information removed from your credit report.

Your Name
Address
Phone Number
Social Security Number

Date
Address of Credit Bureau

Re: Incorrect information on credit report

Dear Sir or Madam:

I have enclosed a copy of my credit report for your review. The following information, circled on my credit report is incorrect:

(List information from the credit report here, including the account number and name of the creditor.)

Please investigate and change this information as soon as possible, and send me a corrected copy of my credit report.

Thank you.

Sincerely,

John Smith

John Smith

Enclosure

Figure 4-2

Sample letter to the credit bureau to have incorrect information removed from your credit report.

Your Name
Address
Phone Number
Social Security Number

Date
Address of Credit Bureau

Re: Outdated information on credit report

Dear Sir or Madam:

I have enclosed a copy of my credit report for your review. The following information, circled on my credit report is outdated:

(List information from the credit report here, including the account number and name of the creditor.)

Please investigate and change this information as soon as possible, and send me a corrected copy of my credit report.

Thank you.
Sincerely,

John Smith

John Smith
Enclosure

Figure 4-3

Sample letter to the credit bureau to request a second investigation of outdated or erroneous information on your credit report.

Your Name
Address
Phone Number
Social Security Number
Date
Address of Credit Bureau

Re: Second Investigation

Dear Sir or Madam:

I am requesting a second investigation of the circled items on the enclosed credit report. I assure you that this information is incorrect.
Please reinvestigate:

(Place item(s) to be reinvestigated here, including the account number and name of the creditor.)

Please investigate and change this information on my credit report, and send me and updated copy.

Thank you.

Sincerely,

John Smith

John Smith
Enclosure

Figure 4-4 shows a sample letter requesting a consumer statement to be placed on your credit report.

3.   File a lawsuit based upon your rights under the FCRA. This option should only be used in extreme situations, when the negative entry is a major one that is doing irreparable harm to your credit rating. Filing a lawsuit is a very expensive and time-consuming undertaking, so you should be fairly certain that the decision will be in your favor.

Credit Bureaus Are Not the Enemy

Credit bureaus do not deliberately set out to mix up credit files, keep inaccurate or incorrect information on your credit report, or otherwise damage your credit rating. They are simply huge companies with millions of records in their data banks, which makes the potential for computer and human error enormous. Also, they are so big that the process of correcting errors can be slow and unwieldy.

> **According to the Federal Trade Commission, inaccurate credit reports are the main source of consumer complaints.**

The sooner you find mistakes in your credit report and set about correcting them, the more certain and easier the correction process will be.

Figure 4-4

Sample letter to the credit bureau to have a consumer statement placed your credit report.

Your Name
Address
Phone Number
Social Security Number

Date

Address of Credit Bureau

Re: Consumer Statement

Dear Sir or Madam:

I have enclosed a copy of my credit report for your review. The information circled on my credit report has been investigated and I would like the following statement placed on my credit report:
(Place your written statement of 100 words or less here. This statement should explain your situation.)

Please add this statement to my credit report and send me an updated copy.

Thank you.

Sincerely,
John Smith
John Smith

Enclosure

You may be pleasantly surprised. If you send appropriate documentation regarding an error (i.e., a letter from a creditor with the canceled check showing payment), the credit bureau may correct the mistake quickly!

Figure 4-5 shows the credit report correction cycle.

A Useful Review: The Nine Easy Steps to Credit Repair

1. <u>Obtain a copy of your credit report.</u> If you are working with a particular creditor or potential creditor, you can ask which credit bureau he or she works with. But the creditor may not know or may not be sure. In any event, it's advisable to ask for your credit report from all of the Big 3. They will be different reports! That way you will be sure that you are covered, since any creditor will be working with one of these credit bureaus.

2. <u>Read your credit report.</u> Note any outdated, inaccurate or negative information. Decide which two or three items are most vital to dispute, list them in order of importance, and disregard any incorrect but relatively minor items. For example, an incorrect rate of pay or a credit card account which was voluntarily closed by you (not by the credit card company) should be corrected, because these mistakes can affect your credit opportunities. An incorrect job title from a position you held years ago, or the number of years you lived at a past address might not be worth trying to correct.

3. <u>Send a letter to the credit bureau identifying and disputing the erroneous information.</u> Try not to dispute more than 2-3 items at a time. Support all requests with copies of pertinent

Figure 4-5

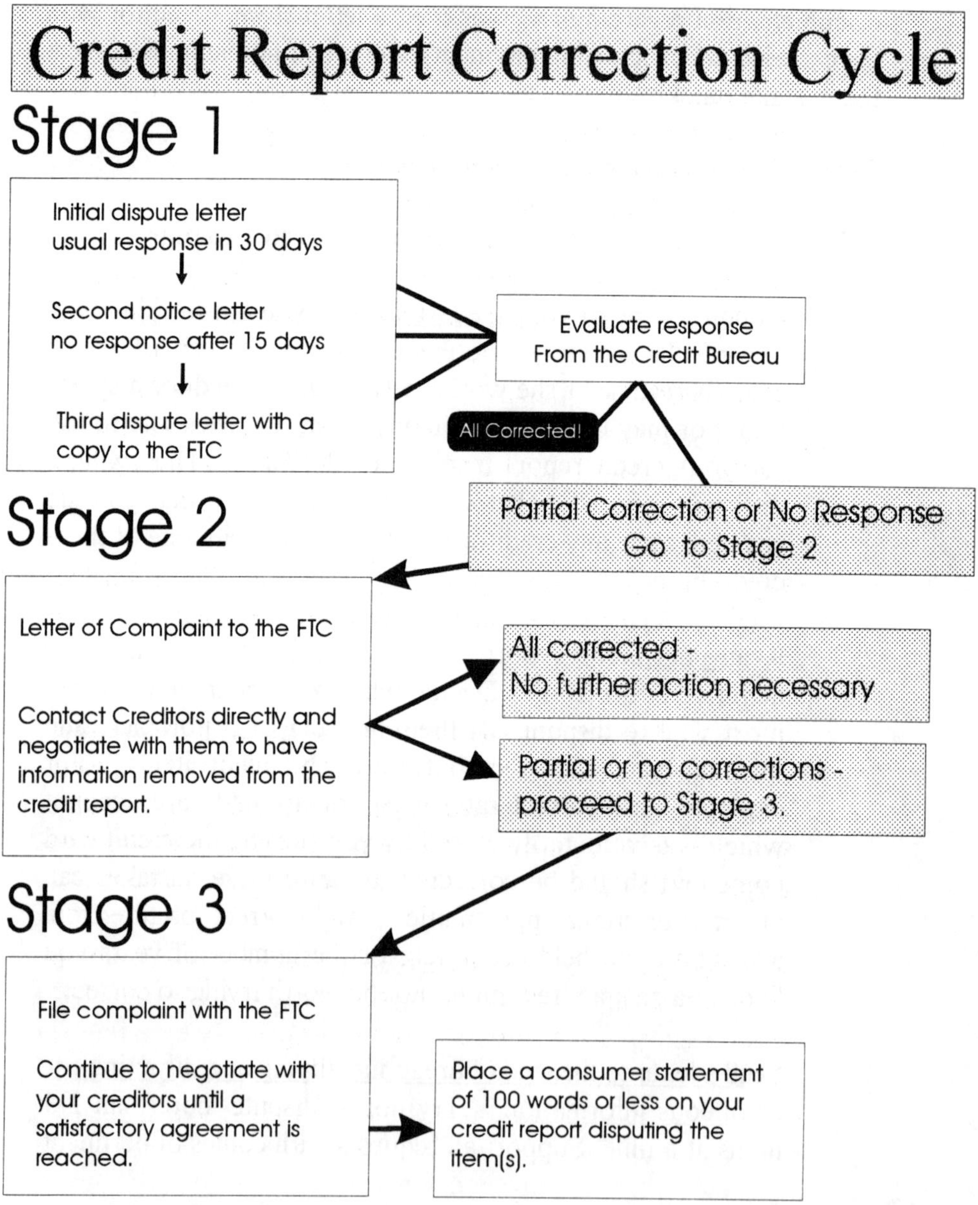

Credit Report Correction Cycle

Stage 1

Initial dispute letter
usual response in 30 days

↓

Second notice letter
no response after 15 days

↓

Third dispute letter with a
copy to the FTC

Evaluate response
From the Credit Bureau

All Corrected!

Stage 2

Partial Correction or No Response
Go to Stage 2

Letter of Complaint to the FTC

Contact Creditors directly and
negotiate with them to have
information removed from the
credit report.

All corrected -
No further action necessary

Partial or no corrections -
proceed to Stage 3.

Stage 3

File complaint with the FTC

Continue to negotiate with
your creditors until a
satisfactory agreement is
reached.

Place a consumer statement
of 100 words or less on your
credit report disputing the
item(s).

documents. Never send the original of any document. Remember to send all correspondence to any credit bureau certified mail/ return receipt requested. Take note: if a credit bureau or creditor can verify only part of a certain item, the whole item must be removed. For example, if a debt of $1,000 is reported and only $500 of that debt can be verified, the whole item must be removed.

4. Follow up on your complaint. Contact the credit bureau after 30 days to inquire if the information has been investigated and, if it did not hold up, if it has been removed.
REMEMBER: EVEN CORRECT INFORMATION THAT CANNOT BE VERIFIED BY THE CREDIT BUREAU MUST BE REMOVED FROM YOUR CREDIT REPORT.

5. Obtain a second copy of your credit report. Check that all negative and unverified, erroneous, or inaccurate information has been removed.

6. Try to work out a deal. Get in touch directly with the creditor or collection agency. They might be willing to delete derogatory information from your credit report in exchange for a payment arrangement. Agreements like this are worked out every day.

7. Get your side of the story on the record. You can add a statement of up to 100 words to your credit report, explaining the situation which resulted in a mark against your credit (a divorce, a layoff, etc.).

8.   <u>Do not give up.</u> If all else fails, you can file a complaint with
       the FTC. Also, you have the right under the FCRA to file a
       lawsuit against the credit bureau (see page 202.)

9.   <u>Apply for new credit.</u> Section Two will show you how to go
       about establishing your credit again.

Remember, credit bureaus are not out to get you! Be courteous and
polite but firm in asserting your credit rights, cooperate with the credit
bureaus, and stay within the law. This is your quickest and most
direct road to success in correcting your credit report.

CHAPTER 5

FREEING YOURSELF FROM DEBT

Being in debt can be frightening and confusing. No matter how serious your debt is, however, you are not the first person to find yourself in this spot. Thousands of people are in debt. And many, many people who were in debt have become debt-free. The most important thing to remember is not to panic. Even in cases of serious debt, such as overwhelming medical expenses, there are people to turn to for help, and there are techniques that can help you get out of debt and embark on a more secure future starting right now!

Debt Collectors
(Surprise: Some Debt Collectors Are Not Nice)
If you have been in debt before, you may already know how unpleasant it can be to deal with debt collectors. Collectors are often rude and sometimes outright abusive. Being contacted at times that may be inconvenient or inconsiderate, being called at work, having a third party involved in the debt, or in any way being harassed or embarrassed by debt collectors can be a real nightmare.

Your Rights under the Fair Debt Collection Practices Act

The FDCPA was enacted specifically to protect consumers from unreasonable harassment by debt collectors.

Your rights under the FDCPA include: being contacted only during reasonable hours; not being contacted at work if you object to this; preventing a creditor from renewing contact with you if you show that you are not responsible for a debt; any oppression or abuse, either verbal or physical, and much more. You should know your rights under the FDCPA. Refer to Chapter 15 for a summary and text of the FDCPA.

Collection Agencies

Normally, creditors will turn over an account to a collection agency or an attorney only if the account is at least six months overdue and they feel that you are not willing to work with them to clear up the debt. If the collection agency or attorney is not successful in getting the account paid, the next step is for a lawsuit to be filed against you.

> In dealing with collection agencies, always do what you say you will do. This will give the agency confidence in you, which will work to your advantage in future negotiations with them.

Lawsuits

For sums under $5,000, creditors can take you to small claims court, which costs them nothing. If they win a judgment against you, you will have to pay not only the original debt, but also the other side's court fees. Clearly, it is in your best interest to negotiate with creditors and pay off the debt. (Of course, this is not true if, in fact, you don't owe the money.)

Why You Should Work with Your Creditors

If you are willing to cooperate with your creditors and arrange terms with them, they will not resort to a collection agency for payment. Once the account goes to a collection agency, it becomes more difficult to negotiate, because the creditor will feel that you have not shown a good-faith effort to clear up the debt. You might still be able to negotiate a lump-sum settlement, but setting up an installment payment plan at that point will probably not be possible. If the creditor takes you to court, you may end up being charged for court costs and attorneys' fees, garnishment of your wages, and other charges.

The best solution is to keep open a dialogue with your creditors and work with them. Be reasonable and polite, but firm, as you expect the creditor to be with you.

If you cannot comfortably do this on your own, go to Consumer Credit Counseling Services (see below, page 46) and ask them to work with your creditor(s) on your behalf.

Not responding to creditors' requests for payment can only cause you trouble in the end, and your financial situation will just get worse.

Looking for Help?

Credit Counselors

Using a credit counselor can be very helpful. Credit counselors can help you assess your total financial picture, set a budget, and make it possible for you to get out of debt. As both mediators and negotiators, they can be genuinely useful.

Consumer Credit Counseling Services

Credit counseling does not have to be expensive. A business-funded service called Consumer Credit Counseling Services (CCCS), the most well-known and widely used credit counseling service in the country, is a boon to creditors and consumers alike.

The purpose of CCCS is to help people who are ready to help themselves get out of debt. CCCS is a non-profit service offering free credit counseling to anyone who needs it. CCCS has offices in every community, which are listed in the telephone book (or see Appendix 2: Helpful Addresses).

CCCS counselors will work with you: they will help you understand and repair your credit report, analyze your financial situation, help you set up a budget, and negotiate with your creditors to make the terms of repayment easier, and generally support your efforts to become debt-free. In addition, they will help you set up a financial plan so that you can stay out of debt.

Debtors Anonymous

Also worth considering is Debtors Anonymous. This group, which uses the principles of Alcoholics Anonymous, is for people who just don't seem to be able to stay out of debt. Check the telephone book for a group in your area, or refer to Appendix 2: Helpful Addresses.

> **Approximately $1 billion per year is stolen from credit card accounts.**

Credit Repair Clinics: Consumer Beware

The Fair Credit Reporting Act empowers consumers to correct their credit reports. Credit clinics, if they are law-abiding, do not have any tools to work with that you yourself do not have. By employing their "service," you are just paying a middleman to do the work for you.

What is more serious, credit repair clinics have been known to employ methods which are disreputable, if not downright dishonest. So if you decide to approach a credit repair clinic for help, there are several things you should be on the lookout for:

- The tactics they use. Credit bureaus are not required by law to respond to "frivolous" complaints, such as the simultaneous filing of multiple disputes in an effort to overwhelm the credit repair system.

- Their knowledge of credit law. Ask a few questions based on the knowledge of credit laws you acquire through this book and see what they know.

- Are they bonded? VERY IMPORTANT. These clinics have been known to disappear overnight without a trace - but with your money. If they are bonded, you might have some chance of getting your money back.

- How they charge: whether there is a flat fee or they charge for each correction. The latter could add up to a lot of money. Also, they might require collateral that you may not be aware of. If so, you could end up losing your house or car!

- Do their claims check out. If they say they can get you credit cards, ask which specific bank they can get them from, then call the bank to double-check this claim.

Consumers should beware of credit repair businesses that claim to be able to "fix" your credit overnight. If they propose to create a "new credit identity" for you, watch out! Such extravagant claims are sometimes based on illegal tactics.

Key Information Should Not be Altered

As we have seen, credit bureaus use key information, in particular, name and Social Security number, to identify consumers. Altering this key information in some way can give you a clean credit history. When you apply for credit, the credit bureau will report that you have "no credit history." However, changing any pertinent information for the purposes of creating a new credit identity is against the law.

Yet some credit repair businesses will offer to:

- Create a new name, use a maiden name or a different spelling of your name

- Alter a few numbers of your Social Security number or apply to the Social Security Administration for a new Social Security number under a different name

- Obtain an employer identification number (EIN) or taxpayer identification number(TIN) and use it in place of the Social Security number

- Rearrange information on a credit application

Once a consumer "owns" this new identity, that person will have to use it for the rest of his or her life.

The plain truth is, resorting to illegal or unscrupulous methods will only compound your troubles. To put false information on a credit application is a federal offense.

If, when you broach any of the issues mentioned above with a credit repair clinic, their answers raise one or more "red flags" in your mind about the reputability of the clinic, trust your instincts and stay away from them!

Should you choose to use a credit clinic or credit repair service, be sure to check with the Better Business Bureau in your community before putting down any money. They can tell you whether they have had complaints against that particular company, and how long they have been in business. The state attorney general's office might also be helpful in determining the reputability of credit clinics.

The good news is that, even when the operation is honest, credit repair clinics usually can't do anything you could not do as well - or better - on your own, using the tools and techniques in this book.

Getting Out of Debt on Your Own

There is no "quick fix" for bad credit or a faulty credit report.

Correcting these problems takes perseverance, but you <u>can</u> do it yourself, legally, and at no charge, if you persevere. The time and effort it takes are more than worthwhile!

How to Handle Credit Card Debt

Let's start with the most common kind of debt, and how to clear it up on your own.

If you are carrying significant credit card debt, you are probably paying a lot in interest charges every month, as much as 18% or 20%, possibly even more, depending on the interest rate used and the method by which balances are calculated by the financial institution to which you are in debt. (For information on how balances are calculated, see page 112.) If your credit card debt is large, consider the following:

- Debt consolidation - combine your debt from all (or some) of your credit cards and transfer it to a single account that offers a lower interest rate. Many cards have special introductory interest rates to encourage consumers to do just this. Some of these low interest rates are even frozen for the duration of the transferred debt. These are the really good deals, since your interest can't go up until the entire debt is paid!

However, unless you are positive that you can resist the temptation to start charging on those accounts again, or you close them altogether, it is not a good idea to transfer your balances in order to free up your lines of credit. If you are sure you can resist this temptation, you are a good candidate for debt consolidation, and it can save you hundreds of dollars per month on your credit card payments. Debt consolidation has an added advantage: you make only one payment per month, instead of several.

- You might also consider taking out a bank or credit union loan, at a lower interest rate, to pay off some or all of your credit cards; you would then repay the bank loan. Again, you will be saving a lot of money on interest charges; but you should do this only if you are sure you will not use the credit cards again, incurring even more debt.

Tips and Techniques for Handling Debt in General

Following are some basic tips and techniques for getting out of any kind of debt, or handling debt when it is unavoidable:

- Save all receipts and keep track of expenses. Fixed expenses (such as mortgage payments or rent and utilities) are hard to change. What you can cut back on are your variable expenses (telephone, clothes). Make sure you pay your essential bills first.

- Put yourself and your family on a budget. If you make coming up with a budget a family affair, the process will be easier and more effective.

51

- Put your credit cards away, keeping only two or three for emergencies. Either close the other accounts or cut up the cards, or both. (If you close the accounts, be sure to get a statement in writing from the credit card company stating that you closed the account, and it was not closed by the company. Otherwise, this may result in a negative entry on your credit report.) See above for information on dealing with these special problems.

- Put your budget, whether weekly or monthly, on a cash-only basis. It works like this: When you get paid, take out enough money to live on for that week or month. (Make sure you are keeping to your budget.) This is a great tool for instant prioritizing of your expenses. You will have to decide what is really important, because if you can't afford to pay cash for it, you won't be able to buy it!

- Think about how you got into debt. Is there a pattern of overspending? Or were there extraordinary expenses that forced you to take on more debt than you could   reasonably handle? Whatever the case, write it down.

CHAPTER 6

SPECIAL SITUATIONS

There are three subjects we have not dealt with elsewhere in this book because they involve situations special enough to warrant a section of their own.

These subjects are:

> ▸ Why you should be careful when you consider cosigning a loan
> ▸ How to handle bankruptcy and its consequences
> ▸ The credit consequences of marriage and divorce

● **Why you should be careful when you consider cosigning a loan**

Cosigning a loan means taking responsibility for repaying money which is borrowed by someone else.

While you will not be the main person responsible for the loan you cosign, you will certainly be responsible if the other person does not meet his or her obligation. Therefore, the decision to cosign a loan, no matter who the main signer is, must be taken very seriously.

53

The seriousness is affirmed by a ruling of the Federal Trade Commission, which mandates that you be given the following notice in writing before you cosign a loan: "You are being asked to guarantee this debt. Think carefully before you do. If the borrower doesn't pay the debt, you will have to. Be sure you can afford to pay if you have to, and that you want to accept this responsibility."

Caution: Approach Cosigning Carefully

▸ In most states, the creditor can collect from you first, without even trying to collect from the main party!

▸ Since anyone who has been accepted by a professional lender would not need a cosigner, it should come as no surprise that as many as three out of four cosigners are asked to pay the loans they cosigned.

▸ The debt, even though you don't have the money from it, might be counted as your debt in your debt-to-income ratio, when you yourself apply for a loan or credit.

▸ According to the law, you may have your wages garnished, lose property, be sued, and have your credit seriously damaged if the main signer defaults for any reason.

▸ In addition to whatever part of the loan is not paid by the main signer, you may also be responsible for additional charges: late fees, collection costs, etc.

Pinpoint Your Obligations

> ► Get copies of all papers related to the loan so you will be fully aware of what you might be responsible for if the borrower defaults, or in case of a dispute between the creditor and the borrower.

> ► Find out what the exact amount of the loan is, and agree in writing to pay only that amount.

> ► You might be able to attach an agreement to the loan exempting you from any additional charges, such as late fees, attorney's fees, etc.

> ► State laws pertaining to cosigners' rights and responsibilities vary. It is a good idea to check the law in your state to find out whether you have any additional legal rights as a cosigner.

Once your credit is damaged by cosigning a loan, you will have to rebuild it, which will take time and effort on your part.

For this reason and all the other issues mentioned above, think very carefully before cosigning a loan. It could damage not only your credit, but your relationship with your friend or family member as well!

● **How to Handle Bankruptcy and its Consequences**

Bankruptcy should be considered only as a last resort. If you simply cannot handle your debt load, this might be the only solution for you. But make certain you are aware of the consequences of bankruptcy and ready to accept them.

Bankruptcy has traditionally been a humiliating and demeaning experience, because it exposes your financial plight to the public and the legal system. As we mentioned earlier, it also stays on your credit report and impacts your credit for 10 years.

What's more, filing bankruptcy is a public act - anyone can gain access to court files and see the legal papers pertaining to your bankruptcy. A bankruptcy notice might even appear in the local papers!

Still, bankruptcy does not carry the same stigma today as it did even ten or twenty years ago. There are actually some affluent people who choose bankruptcy as a convenient way to exempt themselves from many of their debts. Also, where people who have declared bankruptcy used to be avoided by creditors, some creditors today actually target them. They know that consumers cannot declare bankruptcy again for seven years after the last filing, so they will be

> **More people filed for bankruptcy in the United States in 1994 than were graduated from college.**

forced to pay their debts. This fact makes them more desirable in some ways than someone who has not declared bankruptcy but has severe financial problems. They also know that people who have declared bankruptcy may be desperate for credit, so they can charge them exorbitant interest rates. Lists of consumers who have declared bankruptcy are actually being bought by banks and these people are being sent pre-approved credit cards!

Despite these changes in the way our society views bankruptcy, this remains a serious decision with long-range implications for your credit.

The typical bankrupt consumer is still someone who is overwhelmed by debt and sees no other way out. For such a person, bankruptcy will result in credit limitations as long as the bankruptcy remains on his or her credit report.

Who Files for Bankruptcy?

Usually people who file for bankruptcy have either just lost their jobs or have sustained an injury or illness that prevents them from working. Without income to pay their debts, they resort to bankruptcy. Bankruptcy can also be a result of economic trends like the recession of the early 1990's, which forced many companies and sole proprietors out of business. Or sometimes a divorced woman may be forced to file for bankruptcy because she is burdened with debts from her ex-spouse which she cannot handle. (This last situation is discussed later in this chapter.)

> **Credit card debt is the main cause of bankruptcy.**

Example of personal bankruptcy:

The company for which Eileen Richmond worked relocated halfway across the country. Because her eighty-five year-old mother had been in a nursing home for four years, and Eileen did not think her mother could tolerate having to get used to a new place, Eileen felt she could not make the move. Within six months, she had used up all her savings, her debts were piling up, and she had to declare bankruptcy.

Example of sole proprietor whose business fails:

Allen Smith owned a very lucrative window-washing business. However, due to an economic downturn, a majority of his customers decided to cut costs by cleaning their own windows. As a result, Allen went out of business. Unable to pay the debts he had incurred, he was forced to file for bankruptcy.

Before You File

1. Note that you must be a resident of the United States for over six months in order to file.

2. Consider this: You should file for bankruptcy only if your current income does not meet your debt obligations. This means your debts exceed your total annual income or your total monthly credit cards exceed your cash flow. In addition, attempts to arrange repayment of your credit cards or loans have been unsuccessful.

Items Not Included in Bankruptcy:

- non-dischargeable debts (federal, state and local taxes not paid within three years)
- court judgments or restitution
- debts incurred by breaking the law
- any late payments of child support or alimony
- any credit purchase of $500 or more incurred within 40 days of filing for bankruptcy

- ▸ debts not listed on your petition
- ▸ some loans for education
- ▸ prior bankruptcy debts
- ▸ taxes
- ▸ certain debts incurred within 20-40 days of filing bankruptcy

If you forgot to list a certain debt when you filed for bankruptcy, this debt will not be included in the bankruptcy agreement. You will have to pay it.

> **Applications that are incomplete or contain false information usually result in denial of discharge of a debt in bankruptcy.**

If you own a home, you will still be held accountable for the mortgage after you file for bankruptcy. Also, bankruptcy does not eliminate your obligation to pay any judicial liens that have been placed on your house. If you miss a payment on your mortgage, the bank has the right to foreclose.

When you file for bankruptcy, you should be prepared to lose many of your personal luxuries.

These non-exempt properties include:

- ▸ expensive automobiles and clothing
- ▸ jewelry (under a specified value)
- ▸ collections (stamps, coins, etc.)
- ▸ pianos and other expensive instruments
- ▸ duplicate household furnishings (e.g., a second T.V. or telephone)

- second or summer homes and recreational vehicles
- family heirlooms
- cash
- bank accounts
- stocks
- CD's and bonds, IRA's, and private pension plans

You will be able to keep only exempt property, including:

- cars or trucks valued at $1,200 or less
- inexpensive clothing, household goods and furnishings
- appliances
- jewelry (must be under a specified value)
- personal effects, life insurance and public employee pension plans.

After you understand what is involved in bankruptcy, if you still feel that this is the best solution for your financial situation, you are ready to proceed with filing with the courts. Once you do start this process, you should keep complete records, including copies of all correspondence as well as of all legal papers.

The simple procedures in filing for a bankruptcy require only a few hours of your time; however, the system normally takes four to six months to process a bankruptcy.

The Bankruptcy Procedure

1. Get a bankruptcy attorney. You may want to call your local bar association for a referral or contact the bankruptcy court for one. Also, before you decide on an attorney, ask him for a few names of former clients, then call them for references. Make sure the attorney

you choose is not one who will let your case drag on for his own financial benefit.

Beware: attorneys who promote bankruptcy in advertising their services should be avoided. Remember that lawyers always get paid up front, even before the bankruptcy papers are filed. Some attorneys even take credit cards!

2.   Fill out the two-page Voluntary Petition and other papers advocated by your attorney.

The petition will ask you to list and describe:

- ▸ your property(ies)
- ▸ income
- ▸ monthly living expenses
- ▸ debts
- ▸ non-exempt and exempt property
- ▸ property that you have owned and sold or have given away during the past two years

3.   Submit the petition and the filing fee to the bankruptcy court. The court will hold a hearing and determine whether to deny or grant the petition.

4.   You will be asked to attend the bankruptcy hearing. Ninety-five out of a hundred people filing for bankruptcy attend a one-day hearing.

5.   You might also be required to attend meetings with your creditors to discuss any property you might have

that could be sold to pay some of your debts, or any other details about what you can or cannot pay them.

6.   All your past and present financial dealings will be examined, and you must cooperate with the trustee who does this examination.

7.   When you file, the court places an automatic stay on all credit accounts and loans. Creditors are not allowed to collect from you during this time. They may not garnish your wages or repossess your car, cut off your utilities, or attach federal/state-funded benefits (such as welfare).

8.   If the court grants your petition, it takes full control of your accounts and assets. The court will decide who gets paid and the amount.

9.   After your property has been sold, all the proceeds are used to pay your debts.

Different Types of Bankruptcy

Although there are several different types, or "chapters," of bankruptcy, by far the most common types for the average individual are Chapter 7 and Chapter 13. For business, the most common outcome is Chapter 11. (An unsuccessful Chapter 11 is transferred into a Chapter 7 at the end.)

Chapter 7

Chapter 7 is the "Granddad" of all bankruptcies. By far the most common form of bankruptcy for individuals, Chapter 7 liquidates all non-exempt property to pay off your debt.

(If you have personal items that are used to earn your income, such as tools essential to your work, these items cannot be taken away. However, if you have several sets of such tools, the more expensive items can be liquidated.)

The following items pertain to Chapter 7 bankruptcy:

- The court will appoint a trustee who will control your finances. The bankruptcy trustee will repay the creditors as much as possible. Also, the trustee will administer the sale of all your non-exempt property.

- You must begin your repayment plan within 30 days of filing your bankruptcy petition.

The creditor will not be paid the full amount due him. Under Chapter 7, the creditor will be lucky to receive any type of payment, because debtors claim that all their assets are exempt. Once everything is sold and you have no other assets, your debts will be eliminated.

You may not file Chapter 7 again for six years from the last filing. Therefore, you will have no bankruptcy protection for any debts incurred during the succeeding six years.

Popular opinion is that individuals who file for Chapter 7 are wealthy; however, Chapter 7 is also filed by people of very modest means.

Example:

After sixteen years of devoted service, May Dowd had worked her way up from file clerk to a position as assistant to a vice-president of her company. She earned a good salary and benefits. When the company was bought by a large conglomerate, her boss was forced into early retirement - and May was let go with three months' severance pay. The disappointment of losing her job plus the stress of job-hunting in a recession were very distressing, and by the time she had been out of work for ten months, May had accumulated a huge debt. She then had no alternative but to file Chapter 7 bankruptcy.

Chapter 13

Chapter 13, the "wage earner plan," is primarily for small businesses and individuals who still have a regular source of income and who seek to reorganize. In order to file Chapter 13, you may not owe more than $100,000 in unsecured debt or more than $350,000 in secured debt. Chapter 13 is probably the easiest type of bankruptcy, because it allows you to keep many items you might lose under another bankruptcy chapter. However, even under Chapter 13, you will probably not be allowed to keep any luxury items, such as a boat or an expensive car.

Chapter 13 sets up a repayment schedule, established by a bankruptcy judge, for debtors who are honestly trying to repay their debt obligations. These debts must be paid off in three to five years. Sometimes, even attorney fees can be paid off under this plan! This repayment plan must be managed by a court-appointed, paid trustee, who gives you three years to repay your debts, with an optional addition of two more years if deemed necessary. Approximately one quarter of all personal bankruptcies fall under Chapter 13. In effect, Chapter 13 is very similar to working out a repayment plan with

Consumer Credit Counseling Service, with the exception that it is court-managed and enforced. Still, if at all possible, use CCCS instead of Chapter 13 - it will accomplish the same thing in the end, with much less expense and hassle. If you must consider bankruptcy, consider Chapter 13 first.

Chapter 11

Similar to Chapter 13, Chapter 11 is used by people and businesses who have too many assets to file Chapter 13. Like Chapter 13, Chapter 11 allows a business or an individual to set up and manage a repayment plan, without using a trustee. Important: Chapter 11 will cost you a lot of money.

Chapter 12

Chapter 12 allows farmers with less than $1.5 million in debt to create a repayment plan, if the debt was incurred from farming operations. Farmers with real estate debt can avoid foreclosure under Chapter 12 by promising to use some of the future proceeds from their crops to pay their debts.

Chapter 20

Chapter 20, which might enable you to keep your property while settling your debts, may not be filed until after Chapters 7 and 13 have been filed first.

There is no question that bankruptcy is a serious legal procedure. But when the bankruptcy procedures have been completed, you will be in a position to start anew, debt-free.

What's more, re-establishing credit after bankruptcy is not nearly as difficult as it used to be. With good financial planning, it generally takes about one year to reestablish credit through bank loans, department store accounts, or secured credit cards. However, you will almost certainly still find yourself restricted when it comes to major purchases, such as a car or a home.

- **The Credit Consequences of Marriage and Divorce**

Joint Accounts and Combined Credit Histories

Many married couples secure loans and credit accounts jointly. Usually their combined income allows for greater credit.

However, couples seldom think about the negative aspects of having joint accounts. They should be aware of these possible problems:

> ▸   Joint accounts hold both persons in the marriage accountable for the debt. Because both husband and wife are equally responsible legally, estranged spouses often fight over who pays for the account.

> ▸   If the account has a delinquent payment history, both spouses' credit reports will reflect this.

Many people do not realize the importance of a credit report until after they are separated or divorced.

> ▸   When a divorced spouse tries to apply for an individual credit account or loan, he or she may encounter a bad credit report, developed during the marriage.

▸ Couples can avoid this possibility by keeping individual credit accounts, including separate checking and savings accounts.

▸ If you do find yourself in the predicament of having bad credit after a separation or divorce, be aware that you will usually be held responsible for delinquent payments on cosigned loans and accounts regardless of your legal status (whether you are separated or divorced).

What Your Options Are

▸ Make an appointment with a creditor or loan officer to explain your credit situation in person.

▸ Write to the creditor or lender and ask for a Change of Collateral, relinquishing your responsibility in repaying the loan or charge account. This can be done only after your divorce has been finalized and the monetary obligations have been assigned to you and your spouse. Some creditors will not honor the divorce decree and that loan or account will be reported on your credit report until the balance has been completely paid.

Example:

Diane and Tom were cosigners on an account in a furniture store. As part of their divorce settlement, Diane took on the burden of paying the furniture debt. The divorce went through. But Diane was afraid that since Tom's name was still on the account, he might purchase furniture for his new apartment for which she would be responsible.

Diane asked the creditors to take Tom's name off the charge account, but the creditors refused regardless of the divorce decree. The only option that Diane had was to close the account and pay off the balance. If she wanted to, Diane could then open her own individual account with the furniture store.

Example:

Sally and Dan recently divorced and Sally moved from California to Florida. Sally chose not to take her car, which was in both her name and Dan's. The car still had a balance due with the bank. In their divorce settlement, Dan decided to keep the car. Sally needed to get the responsibility of the loan placed on Dan solely, so she requested a change of collateral. The bank approved the change and held Dan solely responsible for the car, but the loan would still be listed on Sally's credit report because it had not yet been paid off. Sally wrote a statement to be placed on her credit report: "Western Bank executed a Change of Collateral for me on 1-30-94. My ex-husband is now solely responsible for this debt."

If you are facing a similar situation, you will need to grin and bear it until the accounts are closed and hope that your estranged spouse pays off the account in a timely way so your credit history is undamaged.

Figure 6-1 shows a typical change of collateral request letter.

Figure 6-2 shows a sample letter from a lender confirming a requested change of collateral.

Once you have dealt with your financial setback, whatever its size or shape, your next step is to start over. Section Two is all about how to do that - the right way.

Figure 6-1

Sample Request For Change of Collateral

Your Name
Address
Phone Number
Social Security Number

Date

Address of Bank or Creditor

Re: Change of Collateral

Dear Sir or Madam:

I am recently divorced and have been granted through the court exclusion from loans #AS123459 and #AS678990. My estranged spouse is solely responsible for these loans. I am requesting a change of collateral.

Enclosed is a copy of my divorce decree stating that I am no longer responsible for the above-mentioned loans.

Please call me at your convenience so that we may discuss this matter in more detail.

Sincerely,

John Smith

John Smith

Enclosure

Figure 6-2

Sample Change of Collateral Letter

BANK OF D.C.

21 West New York Ave.
Washington, D.C. 21002

June 30, 1994

Ms. Jane Brown
123 First Street
Anytown, NJ 12345

Dear Ms. Brown:

This letter will serve as your confirmation that a change of collateral for the two loans, A-1234 and B-4567, has been approved. You are hereby released of your obligation in paying these two loans.

If you have any questions, please do not hesitate to call.

Sincerely,

John Smith

John Smith

Enclosure

SECTION TWO

WHAT YOU NEED TO KNOW

TO ESTABLISH AND MAINTAIN

A SOUND CREDIT RECORD

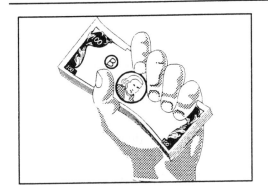

CHAPTER 7

STARTING FRESH

Rebuilding Your Credit

We're going to start this section of *Second Chance* by assuming that you have put the first part of this book to good use. You are now debt-free.

First, we'd like to congratulate you.

Second, we'd like you to make yourself a promise: you are going to stay out of debt.

If you really intend to remain debt-free, this part of the book will show you not only how to establish new credit, but also how to keep that new-found credit on a firm footing.

As the first step in establishing credit again, you can choose either a department store credit card, a secured card, or a bank loan. Remember, if you are turned down by one institution, do not hesitate to apply somewhere else.

We recommend starting with a department store charge account, because that is probably the easiest credit for you to get right now.

Department Store Charge Accounts

A good place to start establishing your credit again is to apply for a charge account at a department store.

Major department stores have different requirements for opening accounts; some have more stringent criteria than others. Large chains that carry lower-priced merchandise are an excellent place to start, because they are likely to make applying for credit easy.

Once you open an account, be sure to make purchases you can afford, because it is of the utmost importance at this point to make your monthly payments on time. Making a number of small purchases is probably a good idea. Most department stores report monthly to the major credit bureaus on all their customers, so this positive information will also go on your credit record. Since it is to your advantage to have favorable credit transactions added to your credit report, when you open an account you may want to inquire if that particular store does report monthly to a credit bureau.

Secured Cards

A second option for rebuilding credit is the secured credit card. Secured cards are easy to get, and are therefore a very good option for people who need to rebuild their credit.

Loans

The third way you can establish new credit is to apply for a loan. All credit is, in a sense, a loan. A credit card is a loan made to you by the credit institution, so you can have money (or goods) now and pay for them later, with interest. A department store credit card works on the same principle.

The main difference between an outright loan and a credit card is that it is much clearer with a loan exactly how much you are paying back - usually the monthly payments plus any interest rate charged by the lending institution. With a credit card, there are so many extra fees that it can be very difficult to calculate what you are paying. This difficulty is compounded by the different methods credit card companies use to calculate your balance - the amount on which they are charging you interest. All this should be kept in mind when taking out a loan or using a credit card. In certain instances, such as a one-time major purchase, a loan might be a better bet than a credit card, especially if you can get a credit union or other low-rate loan.

Loans can also be useful in repairing credit by helping you build a good payment history. The best way to do this is to start small and proceed step by step. The first step should be to open checking and savings accounts at a local bank. After establishing bank accounts, apply for a small loan from the bank. Once you have repaid this loan - making all payments on time and meeting at least the minimum monthly obligation - you are on the road to having a good credit report. It is essential to make sure the bank will report this loan history to at least one of the major credit bureaus, or it will not help your credit record.

Whichever avenue you choose to start rebuilding your credit, it will take time. Most important, keep a close watch on your current approach to credit and make sure not to slip back into your old bad credit habits.

CHAPTER 8

CREDIT CARDS: AN AMERICAN WAY OF LIFE

How the Credit Industry Operates

A credit company operates with one purpose: to make a profit through consumers' use of credit cards.

The credit card industry is a multi-billion dollar business that has grown enormously in the past twenty years. Credit card companies provide many products and services to businesses and consumers.

MasterCard, Visa, Sears Discover Card, American Express, and some department store cards (e.g., Bloomingdale's, J.C. Penney, and Office Depot) provide credit to consumers and businesses. These products and services are offered nationwide and include:

- various types of credit cards with different interest rates and credit limits
- credit protection services

- credit payment services

The larger credit card companies provide these services not only nationwide, but internationally.

> **There are over one billion credit cards of all types in circulation.**

It is a well-known fact that credit cards gross billions of dollars annually for creditors and others in the industry. Credit card companies generate revenue from the fees they charge when a consumer uses a credit card. Consumers are lured to obtain and purchase goods with credit cards through clever advertisements and promotions.

For example, credit card products are widely solicited and advertised to consumers through telecommunications and mass mailings.

Example:

Ocean Bank recently created a credit card with a 14.3 % interest rate. A decision is made to market the card via a mass mailing. The bank purchases a list of pre-qualified consumers from a credit bureau and sends the mailing to those people. Mary Mitchell receives the credit card information and applies for the Ocean Bank credit card. The bank approves her application. Ms. Mitchell then charges purchases to her new Ocean Bank card, and the bank starts making money on her account through interest charges and various other fees.

Credit card companies also offer incentives for using their credit card, such as rebates and low introductory rates. Department stores have also mastered the concept of offering discounts on purchases made with their store credit card.

In one way or another, a credit company's purpose is to sell its credit card to as many qualified consumers as possible, and then to persuade those consumers to make purchases using the card.

> **In the late 1960's, the first big wave of credit card mailings hit the country. Creditors used unverified lists and reports on consumers. Since the lists were not screened, credit was being given to infants, family pets, and even deceased family members.**

Issuing Credit

Upon approval of the application, credit is issued to the consumer. (A "pre-approved" card does not mean your application will automatically be accepted. If your credit report is bad, the "approval" will be withdrawn.) Creditors base the credit limit on the consumer's salary and credit history. In some instances, the consumer sets his or her own credit limit.

When consumers with a history of slow payments are granted credit, the creditor will simply grant a smaller credit limit.

Example:

Sid Walters has a history of lagging behind in his credit card
payments. He applies for credit at a local department store, and his
application is accepted, but his credit line is only $200. This allows
the credit company to monitor the account and minimize their risk.

> **Visa issued 391.2 million cards in 1994, with a card volume
> of US$630.7 billion.**

Credit Cards: A Growing Way of Life

From modest beginnings in the early part of this century, credit cards
are now being used to feed and clothe families and finance
home-buying and small businesses.

Clearly, credit cards are an integral part of life today, and without
them modern society as we know it would quickly grind to a halt.
During the last decade, the credit card industry has quadrupled in
volume, with close to 475 million cards issued as of the end of 1994,
an average consumer debt of $2,500 per card, and total debt of about
3.5 trillion dollars. This growth shows no signs of slowing down.

Industry Leaders

MasterCard

> **In 1994, MasterCard had 45 million cards in circulation, with a volume of US$91.3 billion, and 4.5 million card acceptance locations.**

MasterCard has not only surpassed all expectations in the United States, but has also excelled globally, with an ever-growing presence on every continent as MasterCard International.

Its regular credit card and gold card services remain the heart of MasterCard's business, but in 1993 MasterCard introduced a number of innovations, including a point of sale debit program called "Maestro" and a remote payment banking service for consumers called "MasterBanking."

MasterCard has also combined services with several companies that offer affinity cards (explained below). You can now get a General Motors, Shell or General Electric MasterCard.

The company also increased nationwide acceptance in over 14,000 supermarkets and more than 600 U.S. Post Offices. Also, MasterCard become more accepted by health card providers and pharmacies.

MasterCard has advanced its computer technology and is continually perfecting the Banknet Transaction Processing Network. MasterCard regularly achieves 99.999% accuracy in processing transactions at a rate of 2 seconds apiece. Worldwide, MasterCard approves over 2.5 billion authorizations annually in more than 150 currencies.

Visa

By 1994, 391.2 million Visa cards had been issued; use volume reached $643 billion in 206 countries and territories, and Visa had over 50% of the United States card market. The VisaNet settlement network also set a record of handling nearly 8 billion transactions in 1994 - peaking at more than 1,400 transactions per second. The Visa/PLUS ATM network topped 200,000 with the opening of an ATM in Peru in December of 1994, and currently operates over 234,000 ATMs worldwide.

Figure 8-1 shows Visa card volume between 1992 and 1995.

Where is the industry headed?

The rapid growth of the card industry is accompanied by constant changes, not only in interest rates and government regulations, but also in the types of cards offered to consumers.

Although the core of the industry is still the standard Visa/MasterCard, for revolving credit, or the American Express Card, for travel and entertainment, new variations on these cards are appearing regularly, and are growing quickly, fed by constant consumer demand for new and easier ways to use credit.

Figure 8-1

Visa Card Volume
(in US$ Billions)

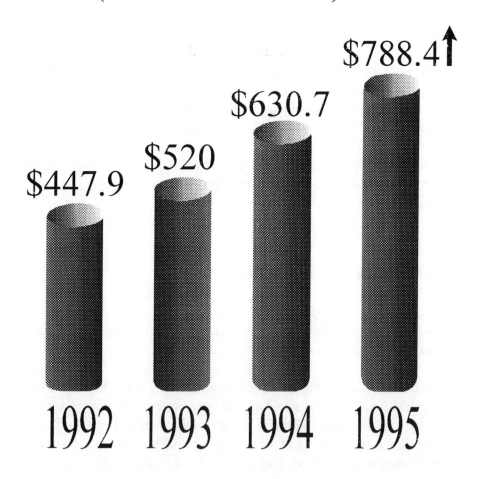

Source: VISA International
Annual Report - 1995

> The earliest form of credit was an engraved ring used by knights in the Middle Ages. The bill imprinted by this ring was presented by the creditor at the knight's castle for payment.

among the fastest-growing segments of this industry are the secured card, the rebate/value-added card, the corporation/small-business card, the debit card, and the affinity card. Each of these cards is attractive to a certain group of consumers - which fuels the growth of the industry as a whole.

The secured card. When it comes to making a decision about letting a current customer fall by the wayside, or refusing business to a potential customer, credit card companies focus on the profit potential in risky consumers. A reluctance to turn down anybody's business has led to the secured card.

Secured cards minimize risk to the creditor from consumers with an unfavorable credit history by having the client deposit an amount of money into a savings account; this amount becomes their line of secured credit. Targeted towards clients who would have been turned down by any issuer just a few years ago - people with damaged credit, no credit at all, or who have declared bankruptcy - today this segment of the industry is growing rapidly. With an estimated potential market of over 20 million consumers, it is no wonder that more and more companies are issuing secured cards.

The guaranteed card. A spinoff of the secured card, a guaranteed card eliminates the savings account, which is an insurmountable obstacle to many people with poor credit. Instead, it reduces the risk to the creditor by having a third party guarantee the loan. The customer then pays the third party a fixed amount per month to keep the line of credit open.

The rebate/value-added card. The pioneer in the rebate/value-added card was the Discover card, which continues to have the greater part of the market. However, new value-added cards are appearing almost daily, spurred on by the obvious attraction these cards hold for consumers. Even affinity cards are offering rebates, if only 1%, because it has been proven that even such a small rebate can greatly increase credit card sales and usage. A small rebate seems to be much more desirable to consumers than no annual fee or other attractions. Frequent-flyer cards, the most common form of rebate/value-added cards, are increasingly profitable and popular.

The affinity card. In 1977, the American Automobile Association initiated the affinity card, which quickly proved successful. Within ten years, AAA had more than 3,000,000 cards in circulation. More recently, the AT&T Universal card has rejuvenated the affinity card market by offering its consumers a 10% rebate on their telephone bill. With close to 50,000,000 affinity cards in circulation, this segment of the credit card industry is still growing. On the horizon is an affinity/value-added card, which advertises the organization name while at the same time rewarding the consumer for using it.

The corporate/small business card. This new aspect of the credit card market is being explored by major card companies. It is not at all unusual for the owner of a small business to receive an unsolicited credit card in the mail, with a pre-approved $20,000 credit line! By increasing the willingness of manufacturers and distributors to accept these cards, the potential of this market can begin to be realized.

Debit cards. Pointing the way towards a truly cashless society, debit cards offer added convenience to consumers, creditors, and banks, by eliminating the unwieldy and unreliable checking account system. Because they deduct money directly from a consumer's bank account, debit cards have the flexibility of credit cards without the bookkeeping and added fees.

Electronic banking. Growing quickly, by the turn of the century electronic banking will be pervasive. Magnetic stripe cards will have been replaced by computer chip cards, and most purchases will be made without the use of cards altogether by using telephone and fax lines or Internet or other computer accounts. The American Express procurement card, already on the market, is on the cutting edge of this development.

The future is already here!

> **Approximately $1 billion per year is stolen from credit card accounts.**

CHAPTER 9

CHOOSING THE RIGHT CREDIT CARD

As we saw in Chapter 8, there are many different kinds of credit cards on the market today - and more all the time. In that chapter, we outlined some of the distinctions between different kinds of cards, mainly from the point of view of the issuer. In this chapter, we will look at them from your point of view.

You comparison shop for a car or a house - why not do the same for a credit card? By shopping around, you can save a lot of money.

To decide on the best type of card for you, you will want to take into consideration your lifestyle, income, spending habits and credit history. The list below will help you be aware of what is available so you can make the most informed choice.

Revolving Credit or 30-Day Charge Cards

Most credit cards fall into this category. These cards have limits on the amount of money that can be owed and require a specific amount to be paid back monthly.

Examples: MasterCard, Visa, Discover Card, department store cards, and gasoline company cards.

Most credit cards are bank cards. This means that they are issued through local banks. Some of these cards are available nationally, some only locally.

What follows is information for you to take into account when you are considering any of the common types of 30-day cards:

Through credit cards, consumers have over $300 billion in purchasing power.

Secured Cards

A good option for rebuilding credit is the secured credit card. The secured card works like this:

You put a sum of money in an account with the credit card company (there is usually a pre-determined maximum and minimum).

You will get a card with a line of credit, usually equal to the amount of money in your account, occasionally a little more. You are no credit risk to the company, since they have your money on hand in case you don't make your payments.

Secured cards are easy to get, and are therefore a very good bet for people who need to rebuild their credit. Most secured card companies will take people with poor credit histories, no credit histories, or following a bankruptcy. Some companies do not request credit records at all. Most, however, require a minimum monthly income.

Since the main purpose of secured credit cards is to rebuild credit, most of these companies report to all three major credit bureaus. Most also offer programs whereby the secured card will automatically convert to an unsecured card after a certain period of time (usually 18 months), during which payment has been made in a timely way. Then you are back in the mainstream of the credit world.

Gold Cards

Gold cards, in addition to enjoying a reputation for being prestigious, carry a rather large credit line (typically $5,000), and usually have lower interest rates than other cards. The standards for acceptance differ from bank to bank.

These cards usually offer special benefits as well: roadside assistance, reimbursement for lost items purchased with the card, travel services, etc. Benefits differ from one gold card to another, even with the same type of card issued by different banks - another reason why it's advisable to shop around.

Rebate Cards

Use of these cards offers the user specific automatic benefits. The most common rebates are frequent flyer miles and percentage rebates usable for a variety of purchases (i.e., automobiles, household goods), cash, mortgage, gasoline, etc.

Affinity Cards

These are credit cards which carry the logo of an organization which has a special interest for the cardholder. Note that affinity cards do not always offer the best rates or other attractive features. In most other respects, they are standard MasterCard or Visa cards.

Travel and Entertainment Cards

These cards are issued by companies (not banks) such as American Express, Diners Club and Carte Blanche. These cards do not offer revolving credit: the balance must be paid in full by the end of each month. Instead of making money from finance charges paid by the consumer, these companies charge the merchant a commission fee for the privilege of honoring the card. In addition, they may not report to a major credit bureau, so using these cards might not be as helpful in building good credit as a revolving credit card.

Credit cards are now available that contain a microchip containing 16k of memory. This is expected to increase to 32k in the future.

Debit Cards

Debit cards are a new phenomenon in the world of credit, having
been on the market only for a few years. More and more banks are
offering them. Debit cards have certain advantages:

- They look like credit cards, but they act like ATM
  cards.

- They can be used with any merchant or vendor that
  takes a major credit card, but the money charged
  comes out of your checking account, exactly as it
  does with an ATM card, and not out of your line of
  credit.

- They have the convenience of a credit card without
  the finance charges, and they are easier to use than
  checks.

Debit cards also have certain disadvantages:

- When you use most debit cards, because the money
  comes directly out of your checking account, you are
  not getting credit. However, some debit cards are
  not deducted from your bank account for 25-30 days.
  In this case, you are getting completely free credit for
  this period of time.

- Another consideration: since this is not a credit
  transaction, it will not help you build credit, because
  it does not go on your credit record.

What Perks Do Credit Cards Carry?

Insurance

Many credit card companies provide insurance benefits to the consumer when he or she uses the credit card. Benefits include:

- Travel insurance. For example, some credit cards provide life insurance for consumers who fly.

- Extended warranties in addition to the standard product warranty.

- A purchase protection plan designed to reimburse the consumer for any damaged, lost, or stolen purchases. If the consumer purchases a stereo and it gets broken en route to the consumer's house, the credit card company will reimburse the consumer for the cost of the stereo.

- Some credit cards offer roadside service for consumers in the event that their car (whether their own or a rental car) breaks down. This service may include towing and other mechanical services, such as roadside repairs for flat tires and dead batteries.

Cash Incentives

Many credit card companies provide discounts on purchases made with a credit card. The consumer can obtain a discount in two ways:

- if a purchase is over a specified dollar amount

- after a given dollar limit has been reached on the credit card

> **You have 60 days to dispute a credit card bill in writing.**

There are other incentives that credit card companies offer to consumers:

- 24-hour customer service

- Free additional cards

- A locator service to assist the consumer in locating an ATM machine

- Emergency replacement cards. We all know the Visa television commercial where the businessman loses his Visa card and wallet; he calls Visa and the card is replaced by the next morning.

- Free card registry service. These have all of your credit cards listed in one file. In the event your credit cards are stolen, you can have them canceled through this service.

- Copies of receipts and detailed billing. Some creditors provide receipts for all your purchases (for example, American Express).

Remember, the first step in using your credit card responsibly is to pick the right one for you.

CHAPTER 10

HOW TO APPLY FOR NEW CREDIT

How to Approach the Credit Application

Your credit application is important and should be taken very seriously. When a potential creditor looks at your credit application, he or she will be looking carefully at several items: are you employed? what is your salary? do you rent or own a home? how many years have you lived in your house or apartment? do you have other credit accounts? As you fill out the application, keep in mind that it is designed to reveal whether or not you are a responsible individual with a stable work and living environment.

Figure 10-1 shows the process of obtaining a credit card.

Figure 10-2 shows a sample credit card application form.

Always tell the truth on your credit application. One good reason is that deliberately placing incorrect information on a credit application is credit application fraud - a federal crime.

Figure 10-1

Process Of Obtaining A Credit Card

A consumer fills out a credit application for a credit card.

The application is sent to the bank offering the credit card.

The bank sends the credit application to the credit bureau to obtain a copy of the consumer's credit report.

The bank calculates the consumer's credit score and determines if the consumer would be creditworthy.

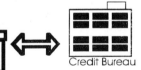

Bank

Credit Bureau

The credit bureau sends the consumer's credit report to the bank.

The bank approves the consumer for the credit card.

The bank denies the consumer for the credit card.

Denied

The bank sends the credit card to the consumer.

The bank sends a declination letter to the consumer explaining why the consumer was denied credit.

Figure 10-2

Sample Credit Application

1. Applicant Please Print

First Name	Middle Name	Last Name	

Address (Street, City, State, Zip)

Home Phone	Social Security Number	Birthdate	No. of Dependents

No. of Credit Cards	No. of Bank Loans	Home ☐ Rent ☐ Own ☐ Other	Montly Rent/Mortgage $

Landlord/Mortgage Holder	Banking: ☐ Checking Acct. ☐ Saving Acct..	Education ☐ High School ☐ College

Self Employed ☐Yes ☐No	Type of Business	Employer

Position	Years with Employer Yrs.____ Mos.____	Monthly Income $	Other Income $	Source of Other Income:

Business Phone	(Income from alimony, child support or separate maintenance payments not be revealed if you do not choose to have it considered for this application).

2. Pleae complete if you have moved or changed jobs in the past two years.

Previous Street Address	City, State, Zip	Years There Yrs.____ Mos.____

Previous Employer	Position	Years There Yrs.____ Mos.____

Has there ever been a Bankruptcy or Wage Earner proceeding filed by any party of this application?
I (we) hereby certify and warrant that the statements made by me (us) in this application are true and correct and that I (we) have read the Disclosures and Notice on the reverse.

X _____

Applicant's Signature   Date

3. Complete if Joint Account

First Name	Middle Name	Last Name	

Address (Street, City, State, Zip)

Home Phone	Social Security Number	Birthdate	No. of Dependents

X _____

Co-Applicant's Signature   Date

Credit Application Plan -

Optional Insurance coverage designed to protect your credit account in the event of death, disability, or involuntary unemployment.

☐ Yes! I wish to protect my credit account with the credit protection plan, I have read and understand the disclosure on the reverse side. I am under the age of 71 and authorize the premium to be billed to my credit card account.

Initial (primary card member) _____

The second good reason is that chances are a creditor will be more willing to give you credit if you are honest and open than if you hide information or provide incorrect answers.

Important: You should get a copy of your credit report **before** you apply for a loan or credit account. It will be to your advantage to be aware of any erroneous information that appears on your credit report. If for any reason you don't want to list some of your debts, at least try to get your credit report and find out which debts are listed there. That way, your application won't contradict your credit report.

Once you have reviewed your credit report, you will be in a position to respond in an informed way to any problem raised by a potential creditor.

Will Your Credit Application Be Approved?

The better you understand how a potential creditor decides whether or not to extend you credit, the more likely you are to get a favorable response to your application.

Creditors have, through experience, determined what to look for in an applicant for credit.

The Four C's of Creditworthiness

The Four C's of Creditworthiness are the key to the credit scoring system.

1.   **Character:** This represents the consumer's ability and willingness to repay his debts, as demonstrated by his credit history. The applicant's stability is evidenced by whether he

97

or she rents or owns housing and number of years at current job and current address. Together, this information will give the creditor some idea about the probability that the loan will be repaid on time.

2.   **Collateral:** This is property owned by the consumer, which he could offer as insurance that he will repay the loan. Having collateral reduces the creditor's risk in giving you the loan, because if you don't make your payments, the creditor can get the property.

3.   **Conditions:** This refers to economic conditions that might affect your ability to repay your loan. For example, if you work for a company which is widely known to be preparing to downsize, this might affect your chances of getting credit.

4.   **Capacity:** this refers to the source of your income and the amount of that income that will be available for repaying your loan. A rule of thumb for a bank loan is that the bank does not want you to be spending more than 20% of your income paying off debts (with the exception of your mortgage).

Credit Scoring

Many creditors make use of a somewhat uniform system to help them evaluate applicants. The process is called Credit Scoring, and it is in your self-interest to understand how it works.

Credit scoring is not only used by creditors to decide whether or not to extend credit to an individual, but also how much and what type of credit to offer. The applicant must have a minimum score in order to be considered for credit. However, creditors have their individual

standards, so you might be accepted by one creditor, even if you have
been turned down by another.

Credit scoring is based on a point system, with a certain number of
points being awarded in different areas; usually between 6 and 15
areas or more are used. The higher your point score, the better
chance you have of receiving credit, and the more credit you may be
offered. For instance, to get a gold card you would probably need a
much higher score than to get a secured card.

Some areas used for credit scoring:

- Monthly income. List gross, not net, unless net is
  specifically requested. Also, the creditor, by law, is
  not allowed to discriminate against an applicant
  because part of his/her income is from public
  assistance (such as Social Security and Aid to
  Families with Dependent Children).

- Age. You may not, by law, be discriminated against
  because of age. If you are 62 or older, you must be
  given at least as many points in the "age" category as
  any person under 62.

- Amount of debt

- Debt repayment history

- Number of years at your current job and current
  address, collateral, number of dependents, and
  checking and savings accounts. The total score
  reflects your overall financial picture.

A sample credit scoring system might look like this:

Area	Qualification	Score
Age	21-28	10
	29-36	6
	37-49	3
	50-62	13
	63+	15
Income	$700-1,000	12
(Gross Monthly)	$1,000+	15
Payment History	Late 30 days	1
	Late 90 days	-1
	Late 120 days	-2
	Never Late	6

Employment	1 year or less	0.00
(number of years at	1-3 years	2
present job)	3-5 years	3
	5 years or more	4
Residence	2 years or less	0
(length of time at	2-5 years	1
present address)	5-10 years	2
	10+ years	5
Bank Accounts	Savings Account	1
	Checking Account:	
	3 items returned in past 9 months	1
	No returns in past year	2
Credit References	Yes	1
	No	0

Debt-to-Income Ratio	28% or less	4
	28%-40%	3
	40%-50%	2
	50% or more	0
Own Home	Yes	1
	No	0
Age of Automobile	2 yrs or less	1
	Over 2 years	0

Sample Scores:

90-100   Credit automatically approved

75-90   Approved unless other compelling information given

45-75   Additional review needed

0-45   Automatic rejection

When Credit is Denied Based on the Credit Score

The outstanding consumer credit card debt in the United States is well over $3 billion.

If you are denied credit based on your Credit Score, the creditor is required by law to tell you why you were rejected. He is also required to give you the name and address of the credit reporting bureau used to obtain your Credit Score. You may then ask for a copy of the report, which is free if you request it within 30 days of being turned down for credit.

Are There Other Reasons for Rejection?

There are many different reasons why an applicant might be denied credit. It is your legal right to know why you were denied, so don't be afraid to ask. The reasons may not be what you think!

What If You are Denied Credit?

The Equal Credit Opportunity Act gives consumers legal safeguards against credit denial. In particular, the ECOA says that:

- The reasons why you were denied must be disclosed to you within 30 days of denial.

- If the creditor does not know these reasons or does not have them, they must tell you where and how to find out the reasons

- If the denial was based in whole or in part on the credit report, the creditor must tell the applicant which credit bureau the report was received from.

According to the Truth in Lending Act, credit card bills must be mailed at least 14 days before the due date in order for the company to levy late charges. If you receive a bill late, save the envelope it arrived in. This is your proof that the bill came late, so that you can avoid late charges.

Tips on Completing the Application

A creditor looks for specific items (employment, salary, and credit payment history) on a credit application and can easily deny credit if the person's information is inaccurate or if the person's debt-to-income ratio is too high.

For example, a creditor will look to see:

- How much you make. It is in your best interest to list your gross salary rather than your net salary. Also list all types of income, including child support, income from rents or dividends, investments, etc.

The debit card, used just like a credit card, is being used more by consumers in the 90's. It immediately deducts your purchases from your account.

- If you rent or own. Owning a home is preferable to renting from the point of view of the creditor, because it shows more stability and resources. If you share a house or an apartment, list only your share of the rent. Creditors look to see how much money you have available after all your living expenses have been paid.

Creditors are also more apt to approve a credit application that is written neatly and where all information has been presented that best represents your strengths. For example:

- When listing your debts, put the ones that have a good payment history first, then list your other debts.

A professional hockey player was once purchased with a travel and entertainment card.

- List all of your debts, good and bad, because the creditor will see them anyway when the credit report is received.

If you have had a difficult period in your life and you have a poor payment history, you can arrange for a personal meeting with the creditor to discuss your situation. Be as honest as possible and show responsibility. The creditor will appreciate this and in all likelihood will be more than willing to work with you.

Example:

Michael Miller is a responsible man with a family to support. Due to downsizing, he lost his job and it took four months for him to get another one. During this time, he was unable to pay his debts. As a result, these accounts were listed as delinquent on his credit report.

When Michael found a new job, he was able to pay his delinquent bills and pick up where he left off.

Then he needed a loan to repair his car. He knew that his credit report had information that would be disadvantageous to him in obtaining this loan, so he made an appointment with the loan officer to discuss the situation. When he heard Michael's story, the loan officer realized that Michael was a good credit risk, even though he had derogatory information in his credit file, and he gave him the loan.

Pre-approved credit cards

Pre-approved credit cards are not always true to their name. Creditors may have some preliminary information on your credit history and think you might be a good credit risk, but they usually request more information before actually issuing you a card. This means that you could still be turned down for that card, if the information you submit does not meet their application standards.

> Credit bureaus sometimes release consumer credit reports to credit card companies for marketing purposes. Those "pre-approved" credit offers you get in the mail are probably a result of this practice.

Credit Discrimination and How to Overcome it

Some groups of people are especially vulnerable to discrimination when they apply for credit.

To protect consumers from discrimination at any stage of the credit transaction - from applying for credit to closing the account - the Equal Credit Opportunity Act (ECOA) was enacted in 1975.

Everyone should know his or her rights under the ECOA, which prohibits creditors from denying or restricting credit to anyone based on sex, marital status, race, age, national origin or religion.

Seniors, women, and students are three groups who might experience discrimination when seeking credit. Being aware of the provisions of the ECOA will make these groups more knowledgeable - and powerful - consumers.

Credit for Seniors

Senior citizens may encounter specific problems in obtaining or keeping good credit. For this reason, they enjoy special protection under the Equal Credit Opportunity Act (ECOA). Discrimination against senior citizens is allowed only if it is in their favor, or in taking into consideration the length of a loan or elements of credit-worthiness. For example, a credit institution is not required to extend a 20-year loan to someone who is 78 years old.

> **When contesting a credit card bill, try to send a letter (creditors are not obligated to investigate problems over the phone). If you do phone them, make a note of who you talked to and the date. This will help you in the future if you need proof of the conversation.**

Credit for Women

Women have special concerns in obtaining and keeping good credit.

Married women often neglect to make sure they have credit under their own name. The result: if her husband dies or she gets a divorce, a woman can find herself with no credit record to reflect her excellent payment habits.

Divorced women can suddenly find themselves in a credit predicament. They may either have no credit record at all, if their credit was under their husband's name, or they can have huge bills under a joint account, which they are responsible for paying even though their husband made the purchases or took the cash advances. These accounts can be very hard to settle and, if a woman's ex-husband refuses to pay, a divorcee may very well have no choice but to pay the bills.

Before you find yourself in either of these unpleasant circumstances:

- Find out whether or not you have a credit history under your own name.

- If you do not, start building a credit file now. This can be done by opening a credit account in your own name, or by asking your creditors to list your name as well as your husband's on your joint account.

- If you have been recently married or divorced, and you changed your name, make sure your name is changed on your charge accounts and credit cards.

Single women with no credit history can also face challenges when they apply for credit for the first time. They should: take out a small loan with a local bank; or open a department store charge account; or apply for a secured card. Within a year or so of prompt payment, they should be able to get a regular credit card.

Women's credit rights are protected not only under the Equal Credit Opportunity Act (ECOA) but also under the Fair Credit Reporting Act (FCRA), which protects consumer privacy and the accuracy of credit reports. If you experience discrimination in obtaining credit because you are a woman, assert your rights under these laws.

Credit for Students

College students are the target of aggressive marketing campaigns by
credit card companies. Students and their parents need to be aware
of these campaigns as well as their pros and cons.

On the negative side, college students usually have little or no
income. Why then are they solicited for credit cards? The apparent
reasoning is that they will use the cards - possibly even irresponsibly -
racking up big balances. When they are unable to pay, their parents
will pitch in and pay the bills for them. This situation is made even
worse by the high interest rates usually charged for college students'
cards.

On the positive side, these cards are easy to get. If the student can
be responsible in using the card - not charging more on it than he or
she is able to pay - student cards are a good deal.

Ironically, credit cards can be much harder to obtain after the
student has graduated and has a job, but no credit history.   A student
card, used properly, will help build a good credit history, facilitating
the graduate in getting other cards.

A word to parents of college students: make sure to find out
whether your child has signed up for a credit card. If he has, you
might be held responsible if he can't pay!

Getting new credit is only half the job. Now you want to learn just
what happens every time you use it.

CHAPTER 11

*HOW TO
MANAGE
CREDIT CARD
COSTS*

What Does a Credit Card Really Cost?

Your credit card costs consist of many different factors: interest rates, the methods used to calculate the balance, annual fees, whether or not you use the grace period, cash advance fees, late fees, and any additional fees charged by your credit card company.

In fact, there are so many different variables that it takes considerable know-how and diligence to figure out exactly how much you are paying for the privilege of using a particular credit card.

In this chapter, we explain these various costs as well as the different methods of calculating balances. Understanding this "fine print" in your credit card agreement will make you a credit-wise consumer.

111

How Balances are Calculated

Several different methods are used by credit issuers to determine interest charges on your account each month. The method used must, by law, be explained in your monthly billing statement. What difference does it make to you which method is used? Even with an unvarying pattern of purchases and payments, the interest charge can vary greatly, **depending on the method used to calculate the balance**. An unfavorable method can result in an effective interest charge of 30% or more!

With all methods, the calculated balance X interest rate = interest charge.

The average daily balance, used in some of these methods, is calculated by taking the unpaid balance on an account for each day in the billing cycle and dividing the total by the number of days in the billing cycle.

Example:

Your balance on October 31 was $900. (Your billing cycle begins on November 1.) You made a payment of $350 on November 13, and made a purchase of $175 on November 15. Your average daily balance (including new purchases) will be calculated as follows:

$$\frac{(\$900 \times 13 \text{ days}) + (\$550 \times 2 \text{ days}) + \$725 \times 15)}{30 \text{ days}} = \$789.17$$

This is your average daily balance.

Methods used to calculate the balance are:

Adjusted Balance:

- Your balance at the beginning of the billing cycle is used, minus any payments made during the cycle (not including new purchases).

- This method is the least expensive for the consumer.

Example:

Your balance on October 31 was $900. (Your billing cycle begins on November 1.) You made a payment of $350 on November 13, and made a charge of $175 on November 15. Your statement of November 30 will reflect interest charged to you on your balance of $550 (your balance as of November 13) minus your payment made before the billing cycle cutoff date of November 30. The charge of November 15 will not be included in the interest charge calculation.

Previous Balance:

- Your balance at the beginning of the billing cycle is used to calculate interest, plus any purchases and minus any payments made during this billing cycle.

Example:

Using the same opening balance, payment, and purchases as in the previous example, your statement of November 30 will reflect interest charged to you on your balance of $725 (your balance as of

November 13 + $175 = $725). The charge of November 15, as you
can see, is included in the interest charge calculation.

Average Daily Balance, including new purchases:

- Your balances for each day in the billing cycle,
  including new purchases and minus payments, are
  calculated and that number is divided by the number
  of days in the cycle. This method is the most
  commonly used by financial institutions.

Example:

Using the same figures as in the preceding example, your statement
of November 30 will reflect your average daily balance (see above for
explanation of average daily balance) for the period November 1
through November 30, including your payment and your purchase.

Average Daily Balance, excluding new purchases:

- This method works like the previous method, with
  the difference that new purchases are not included in
  arriving at the average daily balance.

Example:

Using the same figures as above, your statement of November 30 will
reflect your average daily balance (see above for explanation of
average daily balance) for the period November 1 through November
30, including the payment but not including the purchase.

Ending Balance:

- The balance at the end of the billing cycle is used to calculate interest. The carryover balance from the previous month is added to purchases made during the last billing cycle, minus any payments made. The remaining balance is used to determine the finance charge.

True Actuarial Daily Balance:

- The average daily balance for each day is calculated by adding any purchases and credits to the current unpaid balance. These daily balances are added together and the sum is divided by the number of days in the billing cycle. This is the method most often used for cash advances.

Two-Cycle Average Daily Balance, including new purchases:

- The average daily balances for two billing cycles are used to compute the finance charge. Payments are taken into account, and new purchases are included. This method is the most expensive for the consumer.

Two-Cycle Average Daily Balance, excluding new purchases:

- This method works like the previous method, with the difference that new purchases are not included.

Other factors used in calculating the finance charges on your credit
cards are: the different kinds of annual percentage rate; all the fees
involved in using your card for purchases or cash advances; and the
cards' grace period.

Annual Percentage Rate (APR)

- The APR, or the interest rate, is the finance charge
  stated as an annual percentage (instead of as a
  monthly fee). In other words, the finance charge tells
  you how much you have to pay in a dollar amount
  for the use of credit, and the APR tells you how much
  you have to pay in a percentage amount each year
  for the same credit. These are not two separate
  charges; rather, they are the same charge expressed
  two different ways.

According to the Electronic Funds Transfer Act (EFTA),
your liability for charges on a lost or stolen ATM card is a
maximum of $50, if you report the loss or theft within two
business days. After two days, you will be liable for $500.

Example:

If you borrow $500 for one year, you are paying $50 in interest plus
a $5 service charge, and you are making monthly payments from the
time you borrow the money, your total finance charge would be $55,
which is an APR of 18%.

- The Truth in Lending Act states that by law any company offering credit must disclose in writing what they are charging for the APR and the finance charge.

- This was made law so that the consumer can tell what will be charged for the use of the credit and so the cost of one credit card, or one type of credit can easily be compared to another.

Consider the difference in the total dollar amount paid for the following loans:

	APR	Length of Loan	Monthly Payment	Total Finance Charge	Total in Payments
Creditor A	14%	3 years	$205.07	$1,382.52	$7,382.52
Creditor B	14%	4 years	$163.96	$1,870.08	$7.870.08
Creditor C	15%	4 years	$166.98	$2,015.04	$8.015.04

Whether you would choose loan (or credit card) A or B would depend on how much you are able to pay back per month. Obviously, Loan C would not be a good option, unless it was the only one you could get.

Different types of APR:

Variable Rates

- Variable rates are tied to the prime rate or the Treasury Bill rate, so they change periodically.

Fixed Rates

- Fixed rates are not tied to the prime rates or the Treasury Bill rate. They therefore remain the same for a much longer period of time than variable rates.

Tiered Rates

- Tiered rates are based on the amount of the customer's outstanding balance or other variables (the more you owe, the lower the rate). Tiered rates often result in lower rates for some customers.

Additional Fees

Other fees to be aware of when you sign up for a credit card:

Annual Fee

Most credit card companies charge a flat yearly fee for using the card, like a membership fee. Annual fees can go up to $60 or more per card. The fee may be waived upon request, and is often automatically waived for the first year you have the card.

Some companies find it good business not to charge an annual fee at all.

Cash Advance Fees

Most credit card companies charge extra fees for obtaining a cash advance - getting cash with your credit card, either from a teller in the bank or from an ATM.

These fees are usually around $2 per transaction, or they may be expressed as a percentage of the amount advanced (usually 2%). The fees can be higher, however. Some companies, on the other hand, do not charge a fee at all for this service.

With cash advances, there is no grace period: your interest charges will begin as soon as the transaction takes place.

MasterCard has reported a 50% increase in cash advances within the last two years.

Different balance calculation methods are sometimes used for cash advances than are used for purchases. Ask your credit card company or read the fine print in your credit application to find out whether this is true for your credit card.

Example:

If your card carries a cash advance fee of 2% and you take out $200 at an ATM using your credit card, you will automatically be charged a $4.00 fee in addition to any other finance charges.

The cash advance fee is stated in the "Disclosure" section of the credit card application; and, if you are likely to be using this service, should be taken into account when shopping for the best credit card.

Late Fees

Most credit card companies charge extra fees if a payment is made after the due date. These fees are usually around $15, but may be $18 or more. The late fee is disclosed in the fine print of the credit application.

Grace Period

The grace period (also referred to as the free period) is a specific number of days (usually 25 to 30) from the date a transaction is posted until you start paying interest on that transaction. It must be law be stated in the disclosure section of the credit card application.

What the grace period means: if you pay off your balance in full each month, you will never have to pay interest on your credit card - excellent news for those who use credit merely as a convenience and do not carry a balance from month to month.

Example:

If you charge a $65.00 item on your credit card, and you have a grace period of 25 days, regardless of the interest rate on your card you will only have to pay back $65.00, if you pay it within 25 days of when the transaction was posted.

If you intend to pay your balance in full each month, the length of the grace period is more important to you than the interest rate.

Low-Cost Credit

Here are some pointers for keeping your credit costs as low as possible:

1.   Find a card with no annual fee, or negotiate with the company to waive the fee.

2.   Look for a card with the lowest available cash advance and late fees.

3.   Pay your balance in full each month, during the grace period. This is just like getting free credit for 25 to 30 days.

4.   If you do carry a balance from month to month, look for the lowest interest rate card. If you can qualify, get one with an interest rate of less than 10%.

5.   Read the fine print on your credit card application. In particular, check out the method of calculating balances (see pp. 112-116 earlier in this chapter).

Some of these methods are particularly costly, and
can increase your monthly payment considerably.

6.   Use your credit union, if you have one. Most credit
      unions offer affinity cards at much lower interest rates
      than their commercial counterparts. When making a
      sizeable purchase, it is often wiser to take out a credit
      union loan than to use a credit card. Credit Union
      loans are less expensive than credit cards in the long
      run.

7.   Consider taking out a loan against your life insurance
      policy, if available. These loans carry the lowest
      interest rates in the industry- - some still as low as
      5%!

8.   Beware the allure of rebate cards and "prestige" cards
      - gold cards, Carte Blanche, etc. The rebate or
      prestige may be very attractive, but what are you
      paying for it? Again, read the fine print before you
      sign. Besides, with the proliferation of gold cards on
      the market, these cards are not as impressive as they
      were ten years ago.

Checklist for Shopping for Credit Cards

√   Grace period
√   Annual fee
√   Method of calculating balances (VERY
     IMPORTANT)
√   Cash advance fee
√   Interest rate

- √ Over-limit fee
- √ Late payment fee/rate
- √ Any other fee

Checklist for Shopping for Any Other Type of Credit or a Loan

- √ Interest rate
- √ Late payment fee/penalty
- √ Early payment penalty
- √ Any other fee/penalty

Disputing Credit Card Charges

The Fair Credit Billing Act (FCBA) gives consumers legal protection against erroneous credit card bills. (See page 219 for a summary and the full text of this act.)

However, even with this legal coverage, you must still know how to use the system to get a satisfactory settlement from a creditor.

What You Must Do:

- You have identified an error. Photocopy your bill and receipt and send them to the credit card company with a letter disputing the charge. (Keeping all receipts for at least a year is an excellent habit to develop.) This must be sent within 60 days after you received the first bill which contained the error.

  Phoning the creditor will not help you with the legal process.

- Include in your dispute letter your name and account number, a statement that the bill contains a billing error, the amount that being disputed, and why you think there is a mistake.

- As with any important correspondence concerning your credit, send the dispute letter by certified mail, return receipt requested, so that you will have proof of the correspondence if you need it.

- You have the right to withhold payment of the disputed amount, including finance charges, until the dispute is settled. The balance of the bill still must be paid.

- If the investigation by the creditor shows the disputed amount to be correct, you must pay the amount plus any associated finance charges.

- If you still wish to dispute the bill, you must tell the creditor in writing within 10 days of the end of the investigation procedure. If the creditor places the disputed bill on your credit report, you may place an explanatory statement on your credit report.

What the Creditor Must Do:

- Acknowledge your dispute letter within 30 days, investigate the dispute and correct the error or explain why the bill is correct within 90 days. You must receive a **written statement** from the creditor that the amount was billed in error, and this amount must be removed from your bill. Any associated finance charges or other fees must also be removed from your bill.

- If the investigation shows the bill to be correct, the creditor must tell you right away in writing that they believe the bill to be correct.

- If the creditor refuses to follow FCBA procedures, they may not collect the disputed amount, even if an investigation shows the bill to be correct. They also may not collect any finance charges.

- The creditor may not take any legal action against you until the investigation process is completed.

- The creditor may not use the dispute against you until the investigation is complete. This includes threatening you with damaged credit, or reporting the disputed amount as an unpaid bill on your credit report.

Lost or Stolen Credit Cards

The Fair Credit Billing Act also protects you from charges associated with a lost or stolen credit card.

Under the FCBA, you may not be held liable for any charges on a lost or stolen credit card if you report the loss immediately. Even if the card is used before you report the loss, the maximum amount for which you can be held responsible is $50.

Although credit card companies have 24-hour telephone service available for reporting lost or stolen cards, you should always send written notification as well, so you will have proof that you reported the loss.

If you lose a credit card, be sure to check your next credit card statements carefully, just to be sure that they do not list any unauthorized purchases

CHAPTER 12

THE CREDIT CARD TRANSACTION

The typical credit card transaction involves several parties: the card-holder, the merchant, the merchant's bank, the national credit card company (Visa or MasterCard), and the cardholder's bank.

Figure 12-1 shows the steps involved in the credit card transaction process.

Let's follow a credit card transaction from the time of purchase until the cardholder gets his bill in the mail.

1.   The cardholder uses a Visa or MasterCard card to pay for a $100 purchase in a store.

2.   The merchant uses a computer hook-up provided by Visa, MasterCard or an independent company to get approval for the use of that particular card for that purchase. Upon approval, the cardholder takes his purchase and goes home.

Figure 12-1

Payment Chart of a Credit Card Transaction

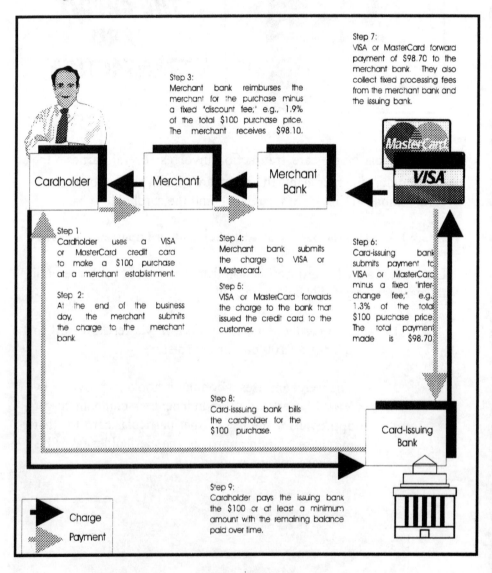

Step 7:
VISA or MasterCard forward payment of $98.70 to the merchant bank. They also collect fixed processing fees from the merchant bank and the issuing bank.

Step 3:
Merchant bank reimburses the merchant for the purchase minus a fixed "discount fee;" e.g., 1.9% of the total $100 purchase price. The merchant receives $98.10.

Cardholder ← Merchant ← Merchant Bank ← VISA / MasterCard

Step 1:
Cardholder uses a VISA or MasterCard credit card to make a $100 purchase at a merchant establishment.

Step 2:
At the end of the business day, the merchant submits the charge to the merchant bank.

Step 4:
Merchant bank submits the charge to VISA or Mastercard.

Step 5:
VISA or MasterCard forwards the charge to the bank that issued the credit card to the customer.

Step 6:
Card-issuing bank submits payment to VISA or MasterCard minus a fixed "interchange fee;" e.g., 1.3% of the total $100 purchase price. The total payment made is $98.70.

Step 8:
Card-isssuing bank bills the cardholder for the $100 purchase.

Card-Issuing Bank

Step 9:
Cardholder pays the issuing bank the $100 or at least a minimum amount with the remaining balance paid over time.

▶ Charge
▷ Payment

Source: GAO

3.   At the end of the business day, the merchant sends
        the transaction receipt for the $100 purchase to his
        bank.

4.   The merchant's bank then reimburses the merchant
        for the $100 charge, minus a fixed "discount fee" of
        1.9%. The total amount received by the merchant
        will be $98.10.

5.   The merchant's bank submits the charge to Visa or
        MasterCard for reimbursement.

**The average amount each consumer
owes in credit card debt is $2,500.**

6.   Visa or MasterCard forwards the charge to the bank
        that issued the credit card to the consumer (These
        Member Banks make up the national Visa or
        MasterCard banking network.)

7.   The cardholder's bank pays Visa or MasterCard the
        amount of the charge minus a fixed 1.3%
        "interchange fee." Visa or MasterCard will receive
        $98.70.

8.   Visa or MasterCard then forwards the $98.70
        payment to the merchant's bank. They collect
        processing fees from both the merchant's bank and
        the cardholder's bank.

9.   The cardholder's issuing bank sends the consumer a
      bill for the $100 purchase, including, of course,
      interest fees, finance charges, etc.

10.   The cardholder pays his bank for the $100 purchase,
      or makes a minimum payment towards the balance.

That's the process, step by step. It takes place millions of times every
day, at banks all over the globe.

CHAPTER 13

DEBT FREE FOREVER

Now that you've got good credit, how do you keep it?

It wasn't easy to get out of debt and to establish a new credit rating. Keeping your new credit rating in pristine condition will also take work. But as your credit builds, you will discover that a good credit rating is well worth the effort!

Keeping Your Credit Record Clean, Step By Step:

1. Get a copy of your credit report at least once a year. Study it carefully. If there are errors, take the steps necessary to correct them.

2. Don't apply for more than two or three credit or charge cards at a time. Every time you apply, the resulting inquiry from the creditor is entered on your credit report. Too many inquiries are a signal to potential new creditors that you may be over-extending yourself.

131

3.   Be careful when you shop for new cards. Look for the lowest interest rate, most favorable method of calculating your balance, and best terms.

4.   Cancel any lines of credit you don't use. Remember to get verification in writing from the creditor that you have closed the account. This is important for two reasons. First, sometimes credit card companies are very reluctant to close accounts - they don't want to lose your money. Second, you need to be able to prove that **you** (rather than the creditor) closed the account - otherwise, it might show up on your credit report as a negative entry.

5.   Don't get too close to your credit limits, and pay your bills on time. Also, keep an eye on your debt-to-income ratio: your assets should outnumber your debts by two to one.

6.   Don't use your credit card for luxuries. If you really can't afford something, don't buy it - with or without a credit card. If your credit card becomes a necessity instead of a convenience, you might end up burdening yourself with a big debt. Remember that whenever you use a credit card, you are taking out a loan at a high interest rate. Keeping that in mind ought to help you limit your use of the card and, therefore, your debt load.

Follow these six steps and your credit rating will be a clear reflection of you: a smart consumer.

SECTION THREE

THE LAW

IS

ON YOUR SIDE

CHAPTER 14

THE EQUAL C R E D I T OPPORTUNITY ACT

Summary

The Equal Credit Opportunity Act (ECOA), which became effective in October of 1975, prohibits discrimination in any aspect of a credit transaction on the basis of race, color, religion, national origin, sex, marital status, age, or receipt of income from public assistance, child support, or retirement benefits. These restrictions apply both to individuals and to businesses. Many aspects of ECOA were specifically designed to protect women and the elderly.

ECOA prohibits creditors from discriminating on the basis of certain factors unrelated to credit-worthiness:

- Credit cannot be denied on the basis of sex, marital status, race, age, national origin, or religion. This applies to the applicant as well as to the applicant's business or associations.

- Women may obtain and maintain credit under their maiden name, their married name, or both, if they qualify. It is illegal under ECOA for a creditor to ask your marital status, under most circumstances, and in most states.

- Accounts may not be closed when a woman is widowed or divorced, unless the credit was based on the spouse's income. Also, these accounts may not be closed during reapplication. Accounts must be reported under both spouses' names. Questions regarding gender, race, or religion are illegal under ECOA; however, questions about immigration status are legal.

- Applicants must be notified within 30 days of application as to whether the credit will be granted or not. The creditor must tell the applicant the specific reasons for this decision or exactly how to obtain these reasons. You may find out why your application for credit was rejected by requesting, in writing, the reasons for the denial.

- Discrimination based on source of income - from part-time employment, child support, public assistance, or retirement - is illegal under ECOA. The amount or regularity of such income may be taken into account, however.

- It is illegal to discriminate against the elderly when they apply for credit. Persons 62 or over should receive the same consideration for credit as those younger; however, the creditor is allowed to take into consideration the applicant's age when determining length of loan and collateral.

- If your business grosses more than $1 million per year, the lender must keep the application on file for 60 days before destroying it. You may request that the records be kept for up to one year; you may also request the reasons for the denial.

- Creditors believed to be in violation of the ECOA may be sued for punitive and actual damages up to $10,000; if the lawsuit is decided in your favor, you may recover court costs and attorney's fees. Another course: a class action suit may be filed to recover punitive damages up to $500,000 or 1% of the creditor's net worth, whichever is less.

EQUAL CREDIT OPPORTUNITY ACT

701 **Prohibited Discrimination: Reasons for Adverse Action**

(a) It shall be unlawful for any creditor to discriminate against any applicant, with respect to any aspect of a credit transaction -

(1) on the basis of race, color, religion, national origin, sex or marital status, or age (provided the applicant has the capacity to contract):

(2) because all or part of the applicant's income derives from any public assistance program; or

(3) because the applicant has in good faith exercised any right under the Consumer Credit Protection Act.

(b) It shall not constitute discrimination for purposes of this title for a creditor -

(1) to make an inquiry of marital status if such inquiry is for the purpose of ascertaining the creditor rights and remedies applicable to the particular extension of credit and not to discriminate in a determination of creditworthiness;

(2) to make an inquiry of the applicant's age or whether the applicant's income derives from any public assistance program if such inquiry is for the purpose of determining the amount and probable continuance of income levels, credit history, or other pertinent element of creditworthiness as provided in regulations of the Board:

(3) to use any empirically derived credit system which considers age if such system is demonstrably and statistically sound in accordance

138

with regulations of the Board, except that in the operation of such system the age of an elderly applicant may not be assigned a negative factor or value; or

(4) to make an inquiry or to consider the age of an elderly applicant when the age of such applicant is to be used by the creditor in the extension of credit in favor of such applicant.

c) It is not a violation of this section for a creditor to refuse to extend credit offered pursuant to -

(1) any credit assistance program expressly authorized by law for an economically disadvantaged class of persons;

(2) any credit assistance program administered by a nonprofit organization for its members or an economically disadvantaged class of persons; or

(3) any special purpose credit program offered by a profit-making organization to meet special social needs, which meets standards prescribed in regulations by the Board; if such refusal is required by or made pursuant to such program.

(d) (1) Within thirty days (or such longer reasonable time as specified in regulations of the Board for any class of credit transaction) after receipt of a completed application for credit, a creditor shall notify the applicant of its action on the application.

(2) Each applicant against whom adverse action is taken shall be entitled to a statement of reasons for such action from the creditor. A creditor satisfies this obligation by -

(A) providing statements for reasons in writing as a matter of course to applicants against whom adverse action is taken; or

(B) giving written notification of adverse action which discloses (I) the applicant's right to a statement of reasons within thirty days after receipt by the creditor of a request made within sixty days after such notification, and (ii) the identity of the person or office from which such statement may be obtained. Such statement may be given orally if the written notification advises the applicant of his right to have the statement of reasons confirmed in writing on written request.

(3) A statement of reasons meets the requirements of this section only if it contains the specific reasons for the adverse action taken.

(4) Where a creditor has been requested by a third party to make a specific extension of credit directly or indirectly to an applicant, the notification and statement of reasons required by this subsection may be made directly by such creditor, or indirectly through the third party, provided in either case that the identity of the creditor is disclosed.

(5) The requirements of paragraph (2), (3), or (4) may be satisfied by verbal statements or notification in the case of any creditor who did not act on more than 150 applications during the calendar year preceding the calendar year in which the adverse action is taken, as determined under regulations of the Board.

(6) For purposes of this subsection, the term "adverse action" means a denial or revocation of credit, a change in the terms of an existing credit arrangement, or a refusal to grant credit in substantially the amount or on substantially the terms requested. Such term does not include a refusal to extend additional credit under an existing credit

arrangement where the applicant is delinquent or otherwise in default, or where such additional credit would exceed a previously established credit limit.

702 Definitions

(a) The definition and rules of construction set forth in the section are applicable for the purpose of this title.

(b) The term "applicant" means any person who applies to a creditor directly for an extension, renewal, or continuation of credit, or applies to a creditor, indirectly by use of an existing credit plan for an amount exceeding a previously established credit limit.

c) The term "Board" refers to the Board of Governors of the Federal Reserve System.

(d) The term "credit" means the right granted by a creditor to a debtor to defer payment of debt or to incur debts and defer its payment or to purchase property or services and defer payment therefor.

(e) The term "creditor" means any person who regularly extends, renews, or continues credit; any person who regularly arranges for the extension, renewal, or continuation of credit; or any assignee of an original creditor who participates in the decision to extend, renew, or continue credit.

(f) The term "person" means a natural person, a corporation, government or governmental subdivision or agency, trust, estate, partnership, cooperative, or association.

(g) Any reference to any requirement imposed under this title or any provision thereof includes reference to the regulations of the Board under this title or the provision thereof in question.

(a) The Board shall prescribe regulations to carry out the purposes of this title. These regulations may contain but are not limited to such classifications, differentiations, or other provision, and may provide for such adjustments and exceptions for any class of transactions, as in the judgment of the Board are necessary or proper to effectuate the purposes of this title, to prevent circumvention or evasion thereof, or to facilitate or substantiate compliance therewith. Such regulations shall be prescribed as soon as possible after the date of enactment of this Act, but in no event later than the effective date of this Act. In particular, such regulations may exempt from one or more of the provisions of this title any class of transactions not primarily for personal, family, or household purposes, if the Board makes an express finding that the application of such provision or provisions would not contribute substantially to carrying out the purposes of this title.

(b) The Board shall establish a Consumer Advisory Council to advise and consult with it in the exercise of its functions under the Consumer Credit Protection Act and to advise and consult with it in the exercise of its functions under the Consumer Credit Protection Act and to advise and consult with it concerning other consumer related matters it may place before the council. In appointing the members of the Council, the Board shall seek to achieve a fair representation of the interests of creditors and consumers.

The Council shall meet from time to time at the call of the Board. Members of the Council who are not regular full-time employees of the United States shall, while attending meetings of such Council, be entitled to receive compensation at a rate fixed by the Board, but not exceeding $100 per day, including travel time. Such members may be allowed travel expenses, including transportation and subsistence, while away from their homes or regular place of business.

704 **Administrative Enforcement**

(a) Compliance with the requirements imposed under this title shall be enforced under:

(1) Section 8 of the Federal Deposit Insurance Act, in the case of -

(A) national banks, by the Comptroller of the Currency,

(B) member banks of the Federal Reserve System (other than national banks), by the Board,

C) banks insured by the Federal Deposit Insurance Corporation (other than members of the Federal Reserve System), by the Board of Directors of the Federal Deposit Insurance Corporation.

(2) Section 5(d) of the Home Owners Loan Act of 1933, section 407 of the National Housing Act, and sections 6(I) and 17 of the Federal Home Loan Bank Act, by the Federal Home Loan Bank Board (acting directly or through the Federal Savings and Loan Insurance Corporation), in the case of any institution subject to any of those provisions.

(3) The Federal Credit Union Act, by the Administrator of the National Credit Union Administration with respect to any Federal Credit Union.

(4) The Acts to regulate commerce by the Interstate Commerce
Commission with respect to any common carrier subject to those
Acts.

(5) The Federal Aviation Act of 1958, by the Civil Aeronautics
Board with respect to any air carrier or foreign air carrier subject to
that Act.

(6) The Packers and Stockyards Act of 1921 (except as provided in
section 406 of the Act), by the Secretary of Agriculture with respect
to any activities subject to that Act.

(7) The Farm Credit Act of 1971, by the Farm Credit Administration
with respect to any Federal land bank, Federal land bank association,
Federal intermediate credit bank, and production credit association;

(8) The Securities Exchange Act of 1934, by the Securities and
Exchange Commission with respect to brokers and dealers; and

(9) The Small Business Investment Act of 1958, by the Small
Business Administration, with respect to small business investment
companies.

(b) For the purpose of the exercise by an agency referred to in
subsection (a) of its power under any Act referred to in that
subsection, a violation of any requirement imposed under this title
shall be deemed to be a violation of a requirement imposed under that
Act. In addition to its powers under any provision of law specifically
referred to in subsection (a), each of the agencies referred to in that
subsection may exercise for the purpose of enforcing compliance
with any requirement imposed under this title, any other authority
conferred on it by law. The exercise of the authorities of any of the

agencies referred to in subsection (a) for the purpose of enforcing compliance with any requirement imposed under this title shall in no way preclude the exercise of such authorities for the purpose of enforcing compliance with any other provision of law not relating to the prohibition of discrimination on the basis of sex or marital status with respect to any aspect of a credit transaction.

705 Relation to State Laws

(a) A request for the signature of both parties to a marriage for the purpose of creating a valid lien, passing clear title, waiving inchoate rights to a property, or assigning earnings, shall not constitute discrimination under this title: Provided, however, that this provision shall not be construed to permit a creditor to take sex or marital status into account in connection with the evaluation of creditworthiness of any applicant.

(b) Consideration or application of State property laws directly or indirectly affecting creditworthiness shall not constitute discrimination for purposes of this title.

c) Any provision of State law which prohibits the separate extension of consumer credit to each party to a marriage shall not apply in any case where each party to a marriage voluntarily applies for a separate credit from the same creditor: Provided, that in any case where such a State law is so preempted, each party to the marriage shall be solely responsible for the debt so contracted.

(d) When each party to a marriage separately and voluntarily applies for and obtains separate credit accounts with the same creditor, those accounts shall not be aggregated or otherwise combined for purposes of determining permissible finance charges or permissible loan ceilings under the laws of any State or of the United States.

(e) Where the same act or omission constitutes a violation of this title and of applicable State law, a person aggrieved by such State law, but not both. This election of remedies shall not apply to court actions in which the relief sought does not include monetary damages or to administrative actions.

(f) This title does not annul, alter or affect, or exempt any person subject to the provisions of this title from complying with the laws of any State with respect to credit discrimination, except to the extent that those laws are inconsistent with any provision of this title, and then only to the extent of the inconsistency. The Board is authorized to determine whether such inconsistencies exist. The Board may not determine that any State law is inconsistent with any provision of this title if the Board determines that such law gives greater protection to the applicant.

(g) The Board shall be regulation exempt from the requirements of sections 701 and 702 of this title any class of credit transactions within any State if it determines that under the law of that State that class of transactions is subject to requirements substantially similar to those imposed under this title or that such law gives greater protection to the applicant and that there is adequate provision for enforcement. Failure to comply with any requirement of such State law in any transaction so exempted shall constitute a violation of this title for the purposes of section 706.

706 Civil Liability

(a) Any creditor who fails to comply with any requirement imposed under this title shall be liable to the aggrieved applicant for any actual damages sustained by such applicant acting either in an individual capacity or as a member of a class.

(b) Any creditor, other than a government or governmental subdivision or agency, who fails to comply with any requirement imposed under this title shall be liable to the aggrieved applicant for punitive damages in an amount not greater than $10,000, in addition to any actual damages provided in subsection (a), except that in the case of a class action the total recovery under this subsection shall not exceed the lesser of $500,000 or 1 percent of the net worth of the creditor. In determining the amount of such damages in any action, the court shall consider, among other relevant factors, the amount of any actual damages awarded, the frequency and persistence of failures of compliance by the creditor, the resources of the creditor, the number of persons adversely affected, and the extent to which the creditor's failure of compliance was intentional.

c) Upon application by an aggrieved applicant, the appropriate United States district court or any other court of competent jurisdiction may grant such equitable and declaratory relief as is necessary to enforce the requirements imposed under this title.

(d) In the case of any successful action under subsection (a), (b), or (c), the costs of the action, together with a reasonable attorney's fee as determined by the court, shall be added to any damages awarded by the court under such subsection.

(e) No provision of this title imposing liability shall apply to any act done or omitted in good faith in conformity with any official rule, regulation, or interpretation thereof by the Board or in conformity with any interpretation or approval by an official or employee of the Federal Reserve System duly authorized by the Board to issue such interpretations or approvals under such procedures as the Board may prescribe therefore, notwithstanding that after such act or omission has occurred, such rule, regulation, interpretation, or approval is amended, rescinded, or determined by judicial or other authority to be invalid for any reason.

(f) Any action under this section may be brought in the appropriate United States district court without regard to the amount in controversy, or in any other court of competent jurisdiction. No such action shall be brought later than two years from the date of the occurrence of the violation, except that -

(1) whenever any agency having responsibility for administrative enforcement under section 704 commences an enforcement proceeding within two years from the date of the occurrence of the violation.

(2) Whenever the Attorney General commences a civil action under this section within two years from the date of occurrence of the violation, then any applicant who has been a victim of the discrimination which is the subject of such proceeding or civil action may bring an action under this section not later than one year after the commencement of that proceeding or action.

(g) The agencies having responsibility for administrative enforcement under section 704, if unable to obtain compliance with section 701, are authorized to refer the matter to the Attorney General with a recommendation that an appropriate civil action be instituted.

(h) When a matter is referred to the Attorney General pursuant to subsection (g), or whenever he has reason to believe that one or more creditors are engaged in a pattern or practice in violation of this title,

148

the Attorney General may bring a civil action in any appropriate United States district court for such relief as may be appropriate, including injunctive relief.

(I) No person aggrieved by a violation of this title and by a violation of section 805 of the Civil Rights Act of 1968 shall recover under this title and section 812 of the Civil Rights Act of 1968, if such violation is based on the same transaction.

(j) Nothing in this title shall be construed to prohibit the discovery of a creditor's granting standards under appropriate discovery procedures in the court agency in which an action or proceeding is brought.

707 Annual Reports to Congress

Annual reports to Congress - Not later than February 1 of each year after 1076, the Board and the Attorney General shall, respectively, make reports to the Congress concerning the administration of their functions under this title, including such recommendations as the Board and the Attorney General, respectively, deem necessary or appropriate. In addition, each report of the Board shall include its assessment of the extent to which compliance with the requirements of this title is being achieved, and a summary of the enforcement actions taken by each of the agencies assigned administrative enforcement responsibilities under section 704.

708 Effective Date

This title takes effect upon the expiration of one year after the date of its enactment. The amendments made by the Equal Credit Opportunity Act Amendments of 1976 shall take effect on the date

149

of enactment thereof and shall apply to any violation occurring on or
after such date, except that the amendment made to section 701 of
the Equal Credit Opportunity Act shall take effect 12 months after
the date of enactment.

709 Short Title

This title may be cited as the "Equal Credit Opportunity Act."

Regulation B

Part 202 - Equal Credit Opportunity

Table of Contents

202.1   **Authority, Scope, and Purpose**

(a) Authority and Scope

This regulation is issued by the Board of Governors of the Federal
Reserve System pursuant to title VII (Equal Credit Opportunity Act)
of the Consumer Credit Protection Act, as amended (15 USC 1601
et seq.). Except as otherwise provided herein, the regulation applies
to all persons who are creditors, as defined in 202.2(1). Information
collection requirements contained in this regulation have been
approved by the Office of Management and Budget under the
provisions of 44 USC 3501 et seq. and have been assigned OMB No.
7100-0201.

(b) Purpose

The purpose of this regulation is to promote the availability of credit
to all creditworthy applicants without regard to race, color, religion,
national origin, sec, marital status, or age (provided the applicant has
the capacity to contract); to the fact that all or part of the applicant's
income derives from a public assistance program; or to the fact that
the applicant has in good faith exercised any right under the

Consumer Credit Protection Act. The regulation prohibits creditor practices that discriminate on the basis of any of these factors. The regulation also requires creditors to notify applicants of action taken on their applications; to report credit history in the names of both spouses on an account; to retain records of credit applications, and to collect information about the applicant's race and other personal characteristics in applications for certain dwelling-related loans.

202.2   **Definitions**

For the purposes of this regulation, unless the context indicates otherwise, the following definitions apply:

(a) "Account" means an extension of credit. When employed in relation to an account, the word use refers only to an open-end credit.

(b) "Act" means the Equal Credit Opportunity Act (Title VII of the Consumer Credit Protection Act).

c) Adverse Action.

(1) The term means:

(I)   A refusal to grant credit in substantially the amount or on substantially the terms requested in an application unless the creditor makes a counteroffer (to grant credit in a different amount or on other terms) and the applicant uses or expressly accepts the credit offered;

(ii) A termination of an account or an unfavorable change in the terms of an account that does not affect all or a substantial portion of a class of the creditor's accounts; or

(iii)   A refusal to increase the amount of credit available to an applicant who has made an application for an increase.

(2)   The term does not include:

(I)   A change in the terms of an account expressly agreed to by an applicant;

(ii)   Any action or forbearance relating to an account taken in connection with inactivity, default, or delinquency as to that account;

(iii)   A refusal or failure to authorize an account transaction at a point of sale, or loan, except when the refusal is a termination or an unfavorable change in the terms of an account that does not affect all or a substantial portion of a class of the creditor's accounts, or when the refusal is a denial of an application for an increase in the amount of credit available under the account;

(iv)   A refusal to extend credit because applicable law prohibits the credit from extending the credit request; or

(v)   A refusal to extend credit because the creditor does not offer the type of credit or credit plan requested.

(3)   An action that falls within the definition of both paragraphs (c)(1) and (c)(2) of this section is governed by paragraph (c)(2)

(d)   Age refers only to the age of natural persons and means the number of fully elapsed years from the date of an applicant's birth.

(e) Applicant means any person who requests or who has received
an extension of credit from a creditor, and includes any person who
is or may become contractually liable regarding an extension of
credit. For purposes of 202.7(d), the term includes guarantors,
sureties, endorsers, and similar parties.

(f) Application means an oral or written request for an extension of
credit that is made in accordance with procedures established by a
creditor for the type of credit requested. The term does not include
the use of an account or line of credit to obtain an amount of credit
that is within a previously established credit limit. A completed
application means an application in connection with which a creditor
has received all the information that the creditor regularly obtains and
considers in evaluating applications for the amount and type of credit
requested from the applicant, and any additional information
requested from the applicant, and any approvals or reports by
governmental agencies or other persons that are necessary to
guarantee, insure, or provide security for the credit or collateral. The
creditor shall exercise reasonable diligence in obtaining such
information.

(g) "Board" means the Board of Governors of the Federal Reserve
System.

(h) "Consumer credit" means extended to a natural person primarily
for personal, family, or household purposes.

(I) "Contractually liable" means expressly obligated to repay all
debts arising on an account by reason of an agreement to that effect.

(j) "Credit" means the right granted by a creditor to an applicant to
defer payment of a debt, incur debt and defer its payment, or

purchase property or services and defer payment thereof.

(k) "Credit card" means any card, plate, coupon book, or other single credit device that may be used from time to time to obtain money, property, or services on credit.

(l) "Creditor" means a person who, in the ordinary course of business, regularly participates in the decision of whether or not to extend credit. The term includes a creditor's assignee, transferee, or subrogee who so participates. For purposes of 202.4 and 202.5(a), the term also includes a person who, in the ordinary course of business, regularly refers applicants or prospective applicants to creditors, or selects or offers to select creditors to whom requests for credit may be made. A person is not a creditor regarding any violation of the act or this regulation committed by another creditor unless the person knew or had reasonable notice of the act, policy, or practice that constituted the violation before becoming involved in the credit transaction. The term does not include a person whose only participation in a credit transaction involved honoring a credit card.

(m) "Credit transaction" means every aspect of an applicant's dealings with a creditor regarding an application for credit or an existing extension of credit (including, but not limited to, information requirements; investigation procedures; standards of Creditworthiness; terms of credit; furnishing of credit information; revocation, alteration, or termination of credit; and collection procedures).

(n) "Discriminate against an applicant" means to treat an applicant less favorably than other applicants.

(o) "Elderly" means age 62 or older.

(p) Empirically derived and other credit scoring systems.
(I) A credit scoring system is a system that evaluates an applicant's creditworthiness mechanically, based on key attributes of the applicant and aspects of the transaction, and that determines, alone or in conjunction with an evaluation of additional information about the applicant, whether an applicant is deemed creditworthy. To qualify as an empirically derived, demonstrably and statistically sound credit scoring system, the system must be:

(ii) Based on data that are derived from an empirical comparison of sample groups or the population of creditworthy and noncreditworthy applicants who apply for credit within a reasonable preceding period of time;

(iii) Developed for the purpose of evaluating the creditworthiness of applicants with respect to the legitimate business interests of the creditor utilizing the system (including, but not limited to, minimizing bad debt losses and operating expenses in accordance with the creditor's business judgment);

(iv) Developed and validated using accepted statistical principles and methodology and adjusted as necessary to maintain predictive ability.

CHAPTER 15

THE FAIR DEBT COLLECTION PRACTICES ACT

The Fair Debt Collection Practices Act (FDCPA) governs what a creditor may and may not do to collect money owed him by a debtor.

- You may be contacted by mail, telephone, fax, in person, or by telegram. If by mail, the envelope may not reveal what the purpose of the letter is, whether by any sign, symbol, transparency of paper, etc.

- You may be contacted only during reasonable hours (8:00 a.m.-9:00 p.m., unless the creditor has prior approval from you to call you at other times).

- You may not be contacted at work if you object.

- If you state, in writing and within 30 days of contact, that you do not owe a certain amount, the creditor may not renew contact with you until you are sent proof that you do owe that amount. If you are sent such proof, you must send proof that you do not owe in order to prevent further contact.

- You may prevent a creditor from contacting you by stating, in writing, that you do not wish to be contacted. After receipt of your letter, the creditor may contact you only to state that there will be no further contact, or to notify you of any specific action they might take.

- A third party may be contacted, but only for the purposes of finding out where you live or work, and the creditor may not state the purpose of the call. An attorney may also be contacted.

- Oppression, abuse - either verbal or physical - and harassment are prohibited by law under FDCPA. These prohibitions include annoyance, publication of your debt, and threats. In addition, any kind of deliberate falsification in order to get you to pay is a violation of FDCPA.

- Violation of FDCPA may be punishable by a lawsuit in state or federal court within one year of the violation. You may be awarded damages, court costs and attorney's fees if you win.

FAIR DEBT COLLECTION PRACTICES ACT

SUBCHAPTER V - **DEBT COLLECTION PRACTICES**

Sec. 1692. **Congressional findings and declaration of purpose**

(a) There is abundant evidence of the use of abusive, deceptive and unfair debt collection practices by many debt collectors. Abusive debt collection practices contribute to the number of personal bankruptcies, to marital instability, to the loss of jobs, and to invasions of individual privacy.

(b) Existing laws and procedures for redressing these injuries are inadequate to protect consumers.

c) Means other than misrepresentation or other abusive debt collection practices are available for the effective collection of debts.

(d) Abusive debt collection practices are carried on to a substantial extent in interstate commerce and through means and instrumentalities of such commerce. Even where abusive debt collection practices are purely intrastate in character, they nevertheless directly affect interstate commerce.

(e) It is the purpose of this subchapter to eliminate abusive debt collection practices by debt collectors, to insure that those debt collectors who refrain from using abusive debt collection practices are not competitively disadvantaged, and to promote consistent State action to protect consumers against debt collection abuses.(Pub.L. 90-321, Title VIII, Sec. 802, as added Pub.L. 95- 109., Sept. 20, 1977, 91 Stat. 874.)

Sec. 1692a. **Definitions**

As used in this subchapter -

(1) The term "communication" means the Federal Trade Commission.

(2) The term "communication" means the conveying of information regarding a debt directly or indirectly to any person through any medium.

(3) The term "consumer" means any natural person obligated or allegedly obligated to pay any debt.

> **The Medical Information Bureau, which stores medical information on consumers, will soon be covered by the Fair Credit Reporting Act. This means that, if you are denied health, life or disability insurance based on your medical report, you will be informed and able to check your medical file.**

(4) The term "creditor" means any person who offers or extends credit creating a debt or to whom a debt is owed, but such term does not include any person to the extent that he receives an assignment or transfer of a debt in default solely for the purpose of facilitating collection of such debt for another.

(5) The term "debt" means any obligation or alleged obligation of a consumer to pay money arising out of a transaction in which the money, property, insurance, or services which are the subject of the transaction are primarily for personal, family, or household purposes, whether or not such obligation has been reduced to judgment.

(6) The term "debt collector" means any person who uses any instrumentality of interstate commerce or the mails in any business the principal purpose of which is the collection of any debts, or who regularly collects or attempts to collect, directly or indirectly, debts owed or due or asserted to be owed or due another. Notwithstanding the exclusion provided by clause (G) of the last

sentence of this paragraph, the term includes any creditor who, in the process of collecting his own debts, uses any name other than his own which would indicate that a third person is collecting or attempting to collect such debts. For the purpose of section 1692f(6) of this title, such term also includes any person who uses any instrumentality of interstate commerce or the mails in any business the principal purpose of which is the enforcement of security interests.

The term does not include -
(A) any officer or employee of a creditor while, in the name of the creditor, collecting debts for such creditor;
(B) any person while acting as a debt collector for another person, both of whom are related by common ownership or affiliated by corporate control, if the person acting as a debt collector does so only for persons to whom it is so related or affiliated and if the principal business of such person is not the collection of debts;
c) any officer or employee of the United States or any State to the extent that collecting or attempting to collect any debt is in the performance of his official duties;
(D) any person while serving or attempting to serve legal process on any other person in connection with the judicial enforcement of any debt;
(E) any nonprofit organization which, at the request of consumers, performs bona fide consumer credit counseling and assists consumers in the liquidation of their debts by receiving payments from such consumers and distributing such amounts to creditor;
(F) any attorney-at-law collecting a debt as an attorney on behalf of and in the name of a client; and
(G) any person collecting or attempting to collect any debt owed or due or asserted to be owed or due another to the extent such activity
(I) is incidental to a bona fide fiduciary obligation or a bona fide

escrow arrangement; (ii) concerns a debt which was originated by such person; (iii) concerns a debt which was not in default at the time it was obtained by such person; or (iv) concerns a debt obtained by such person as a secured party in a commercial credit transaction involving the creditor.

(7) The term "location information" means a consumer's place of abode and his telephone number at such place, or his place of employment.

(8) The term "State" means any State, territory, or possession of the United States, the District of Columbia, the Commonwealth of Puerto Rico, or any political subdivision of any of the foregoing. (Pub.L. 90-321, Title VIII, Sec. 803, as added Pub.L. 95-109, Sept. 20, 1977, 91 Stat. 875.)

> **If your credit report has been modified due to your repair efforts, the credit bureau must provide anybody who has looked at your credit report within the last six months with the updated report.**

Sec. 1692b. Acquisition of location information

Any debt collector communicating with any person other than the consumer for the purpose of acquiring location information about the consumer shall -

(1)   identify himself, state that he is confirming or correcting location information concerning the consumer, and, only if expressly requested, identify his employer;

(2)   not state that such consumer owes any debt;

(3)   not communicate with any such person more than once unless requested to do so by such person or unless the debt collector

reasonably believes that the earlier response of such person is erroneous or incomplete and that such person now has correct or complete location information;

(4) not communicate by post card;

(5) not use any language or symbol on any envelope or in the contents of any communication effected by the mails or telegram that indicates that the debt collector is in the debt collection business or that the communication relates to the collection of a debt; and

(6) after the debt collector knows the consumer is represented by an attorney with regard to the subject debt and has knowledge of, or can readily ascertain, such attorney's name and address, not communicate with any person other than that attorney, unless the attorney fails to respond within a reasonable period of time to communication from the debt collector. (Pub.L., 90-321, Title VIII, Sec. 804, as added Pub.L. 95-109,.Sept. 20, 1977, 91 Stat. 876.)

Sec. 1692c. **Communication in connection with debt collection**

(a) Communication with the consumer generally - Without the prior consent of the consumer given directly to the debt collector or the express permission of a court of competent jurisdiction, a debt collector may not communicate with a consumer in connection with the collection of any debt -

(1) at any unusual time or place or a time or place known or which should be known to be inconvenient to the consumer. In the absence of knowledge of circumstances to the contrary, a debt collector shall assume that the convenient time for communicating with a consumer is after 8 o'clock antemeridian and before 9 o'clock postmeridian, local time at the consumer's location;

(2) if the debt collector knows the consumer is represented by an attorney with respect to such debt and has knowledge of, or can readily ascertain, such attorney's name and address, unless the

attorney fails to respond within a reasonable period of time to a communication from the debt collector or unless the attorney consents to direct communication with the consumer; or

(3) at the consumer's place of employment if the debt collector knows or has reason to know that the consumer's employer prohibits the consumer from receiving such communication.

 (b) Communication with third parties - Except as provided in section 1692b of this title, without the prior consent of the consumer given directly to the debt collector, or the express permission of a court of competent jurisdiction, or as reasonably necessary to effectuate a post-judgment judicial remedy, a debt collector may not communicate, in connection with the collection of any debt, with any person other than the consumer, his attorney, a consumer reporting agency if otherwise permitted by law, the creditor, the attorney of the creditor, or the attorney of the debt collector.

c) Ceasing communication - If a consumer notifies a debt collector in writing that the consumer refuses to pay a debt or that the consumer wishes the debt collector to cease further communication with the consumer, the debt collector shall not communicate further with the consumer with respect to such debt, except -

(1) to advise the consumer that the debt collector's further efforts are being terminated;

(2) to notify the consumer that the debt collector or creditor may invoke specified remedies which are ordinarily invoked by such debt collector or creditor; or

(3) where applicable, to notify the consumer that the debt collector or creditor intends to invoke a specified remedy. If such notice from the consumer is made by mail, notification shall be complete upon receipt.

(d) Definitions - For the purpose of this section, the term "consumer" includes the consumer's spouse, parent (if the consumer is a minor), guardian, executor, or administrator. (Pub.L. 90-321, Title VIII, Sec. 805, as added Pub.L. 95-109, Sept. 20, 1977, 91 Stat. 876.)

Sec. 1692d. **Harassment or abuse**

A debt collector may not engage in any conduct the natural consequence of which is to harass, oppress, or abuse any person in connection with the collection of a
debt. Without limiting the general application of the foregoing, the following conduct is a violation of this section:
(1) The use or threat of use of violence or other criminal means to harm the physical person, Reputation, or property of any person.

> **As part of your credit repair efforts, ask your creditor to notify all the Big Three credit bureaus with any positive information, such as prompt payment of your bills.**

(2) The use of obscene or profane language or language the natural consequence of which is to abuse the hearer or reader.
(3) The publication of a list of consumers who allegedly refuse to pay debts, except to a consumer reporting agency or to persons meeting the requirements of section 1681a(f) or 1681b(3) of this title.
(4) The advertisement for sale of any debt to coerce payment of the debt.
(5) Causing a telephone to ring or engaging any person in telephone conversation repeatedly or   continuously with intent to annoy, abuse, or harass any person at the called number.
(6) Except as provided in section 1692b of this title, the placement of telephone calls without meaningful disclosure of the caller's identity. (Pub.L. 90-321, Title VIII, Sec. 806, as added Pub.L. 95-

109, Sept. 20, 1977, 91 Stat.877.)

Sec. 1692e. **False or misleading representations**

A debt collector may not use any false, deceptive, or misleading representation or means in connection with the collection of any debt. Without limiting the general application of the foregoing, the following conduct is a violation of this section:

(1) The false representation or implication that the debt collector is vouched for, bonded by, or affiliated with the United States or any State, including the use of any badge, uniform, or facsimile thereof.
(2) The false representation of -
(A) the character, amount, or legal status of any debt; or (B) any services rendered or compensation which may be lawfully received by any debt collector for the collection of a debt.
(3) The false representation or implication that any individual is an attorney or that any communication is from an attorney.
(4) The representation or implication that nonpayment of any debt will result in the arrest or imprisonment of any person or the seizure, garnishment, attachment, or sale of any property or wages of any person unless such action is lawful and the debt collector or creditor intends to take such action.
(5) The threat to take any action that cannot legally be taken or that is not   intended to be taken.
(6) The false representation or implication that a sale, referral, or other transfer of any interest in a debt shall cause the consumer to -
(A) lose any claim or defense to payment of the debt; or
(B) become subject to any practice prohibited by this subchapter.
(7) The false representation or implication that the consumer committed any crime or other conduct in order to disgrace the consumer.

(8) Communicating or threatening to communicate to any person credit information which is known or which should be known to be false, including the failure to communicate that a disputed debt is disputed.

(9) The use or distribution of any written communication which simulates or is falsely represented to be a document authorized, issued, or approved by any court, official, or agency of the United States or any State, or which creates a false impression as to its source, authorization, or approval.

(10) The use of any false representation or deceptive means to collect or attempt to collect any debt or to obtain information concerning a consumer.

(11) Except as otherwise provided for communications to acquire location information under section 1692b of this title, the failure to disclose clearly in all communications made to collect a debt or to obtain information about a consumer, that the debt collector is attempting to collect a debt and that any information obtained will be used for that purpose.

(12) The false representation or implication that accounts have been turned over to innocent purchasers for value.

(13) The false representation or implication that documents are legal process.

(14) The use of any business, company, or organization name other than the true name of the debt collector's business, company, or organization.

(15) The false representation or implication that documents are not legal process forms or do not require action by the consumer.

(16) The false representation or implication that a debt collector operates or is employed by a consumer reporting agency as defined by section 1681a(f) of this title. (Pub.L. 90-321, Title VIII, Sec. 807, as added Pub.L. 95-109, Sept. 20, 1977, 91 Stat. 877.)

Sec. 1692f. **Unfair practices**

A debt collector may not use unfair or unconscionable means to collect or attempt to collect any debt. Without limiting the general application of the foregoing, the following conduct is a violation of this section:

(1) The collection of any amount (including any interest, fee, charge, or expense incidental to the principal obligation) unless such amount is expressly authorized by the agreement creating the debt or permitted by law.

(2) The acceptance by a debt collector from any person of a check or other payment instrument postdated by more than five days unless such person is notified in writing of the debt collector's intent to deposit such check or instrument not more than ten nor less than three business days prior to such deposit.

> It is advisable that a husband and wife carry different credit cards when traveling. This is because if one card is lost or stolen and must be deactivated, they can use the other card.

(3) The solicitation by a debt collector of any postdated check or other postdated payment instrument for the purpose of threatening or instituting criminal prosecution.

(4) Depositing or threatening to deposit any postdated check or other postdated payment instrument prior to the date on such check or instrument.

(5) Causing charges to be made to any person for communications by concealment of the true purpose of the communication. Such charges include, but are not limited to, collect telephone calls and telegram fees.

(6) Taking or threatening to take any nonjudicial action to effect dispossession or disablement of property if -

(A) there is no present right to possession of the property claimed as collateral through an enforceable security interest;

(B) there is no present intention to take possession of the property; or

C) the property is exempt by law from such dispossession or disablement.

(7) Communicating with a consumer regarding a debt by post card.

(8) Using any language or symbol, other than the debt collector's address, on any envelope when communicating with a consumer by use of the mails or by telegram, except that a debt collector may use hi s business name if such name does not indicate that he is in the debt collection business. (Pub.L. 90-321, Title VIII, Sec. 808, as added Pub.L. 95-109, Sept. 20, 1977, 91 Stat. 879.)

Sec. 1692g. **Validation of debts**

Notice of debt; contents

(a) Within five days after the initial communication with a consumer in connection with the collection of any debt, a debt collector shall, unless the following information is contained in the initial communication or the consumer has paid the debt, send the consumer a written notice containing -

(1) the amount of the debt;

(2) the name of the creditor to whom the debt is owed;

(3) a statement that unless the consumer, within thirty days after receipt of the notice, disputes the validity of the debt, or any portion thereof, the debt will be assumed to be valid by the debt collector;

(4) a statement that if the consumer notifies the debt collector in writing within the thirty-day period that the debt, or any portion thereof, is disputed, the debt collector will obtain verification of the

debt or a copy of a judgment against the consumer and a copy of
such verification or judgment will be mailed to the consumer by the
debt collector; and

(5) a statement that, upon the consumer's written request within the
thirty-day period, the debt collector will provide the consumer with
the name and address of the original creditor, if different from the
current creditor.

Disputed debts

(b) If the consumer notifies the debt collector in writing within the
thirty-day period described in subsection (a) of this section that the
debt, or any portion thereof, is disputed, or that the consumer
requests the name and address of the original creditor, the debt
collector shall cease collection of the debt, or any disputed portion
thereof, until the debt collector obtains verification of the debt or a
copy of a judgment, or the name and address of the original creditor,
and a copy of such verification or judgment, or name and address of
the original creditor, is mailed to the consumer by the debt collector.

Admission of liability

C) The failure of a consumer to dispute the validity of a debt under
this section may not be construed by any court as an admission of
liability by the consumer. (Pub.L. 90-321, Title VIII, Sec. 809, as
added Pub.L. 95- 109, Sept. 20, 1977, 91 Stat. 879.)

Sec. 1692h. **Multiple debts**

If any consumer owes multiple debts and makes any single payment
to any debt collector with respect to such debts, such debt collector
may not apply such payment to any debt which is disputed by the

consumer and, where applicable, shall apply such payment in accordance with the consumer's directions. (Pub.L. 90-321, Title VIII, Sec. 810, as added Pub.L. 95- 109, Sept. 20, 1977, 91 Stat. 880.)

Sec. 1692i. **Legal actions by debt collectors**

(a) Any debt collector who brings any legal action on a debt against any consumer shall -

(1) in the case of an action to enforce an interest in real property securing the consumer's obligation, bring such action only in a judicial district or similar legal entity in which such real property is located; or

(2) in the case of an action not described in paragraph (1), bring such action only in the judicial district or similar legal entity -

(A) in which such consumer signed the contract sued upon; or

(B) in which such consumer resides at the commencement of the action.

(b) Nothing in this subchapter shall be construed to authorize the bringing of legal actions by debt collectors. (Pub.L. 90-321, Title VIII, Sec. 811, as added   Pub.L.   95-109, Sept. 20, 1977, 91 Stat. 880.)Sec. 1692j. Furnishing certain deceptive forms

(a) It is unlawful to design, compile, and furnish any form knowing that such form would be used to create the false belief in a consumer that a person other than the creditor of such consumer is participating in the collection of or in an attempt to collect a debt such consumer allegedly owes such creditor, when in fact such

By law, bills have to be sent at least 14 days before the due
date to enable you, the consumer, to avoid finance charges.
Tip: if you received a bill late, keep the envelope it came in as
proof of the postmark date.

person is not so participating. (b) Any person who violates this
section shall be liable to the same extent and in the same manner as
a debt collector is liable under section 1962k of this title for failure
to comply with a provision of this subchapter. (Pub.L. 90-321,
Title VIII, Sec. 812, as added Pub.L. 95- 109, Sept. 20, 1977, 91
Stat. 880.)

Sec. 1692k. **Civil liability**

Amount of damages

(a) Except as otherwise provided by this section, any debt collector
who fails to comply with any provision of this subchapter with
respect to any person is liable to such person in an amount equal to
the sum of -
(1) any actual damage sustained by such person as a result of such
failure;
(2)(A) in the case of any action by an individual, such additional
damages as the court may allow, but not exceeding $1,000; or
(B) in the case of a class action, (I) such amount for each named
plaintiff as could be recovered under subparagraph (A), and (ii) such
amount as the court may allow for all other class members, without
regard to a minimum individual recovery, not to exceed the lesser of
$500,000 or 1 percent of the net worth of the debt collector; and
(3) in the case of any successful action to enforce the foregoing

liability, the costs of the action, together with a reasonable attorney's fee as determined by the court. On a finding by the court that an action under this section was brought in bad faith and for the purpose of harassment, the court may award to the defendant attorney's fees reasonable in relation to the work expended and costs.

Factors considered by court

(b) In determining the amount of liability in any action under subsection (a) of this section, the court shall consider, among other relevant factors -
(1) in any individual action under subsection (a)(2)(A) of this section, the frequency and persistence of noncompliance by the debt collector, the nature of such noncompliance, and the extent to which such noncompliance was intentional; or
(2) in any class action under subsection (a)(2)(B) of this section, the frequency and persistence of noncompliance by the debt collector, the nature of such noncompliance, the resources of the debt collector, the number of persons adversely affected, and the extent to which the debt collector's noncompliance was intentional.

Intent

C) A debt collector may not be held liable in any action brought under this subchapter if the debt collector shows by a preponderance of evidence that the violation was not intentional and resulted from a bona fide error notwithstanding the maintenance of procedures reasonably adapted to avoid any such error.

Jurisdiction

(d) An action to enforce any liability created by this subchapter may

173

be brought in any appropriate United States district court without regard to the amount in controversy, or in any other court of competent jurisdiction, within one year from the date on which the violation occurs.

Advisory opinions of Commission

(e) No provision of this section imposing any liability shall apply to any act done or omitted in good faith in conformity with any advisory opinion of the Commission, notwithstanding that after such act or omission has occurred, such opinion is amended, rescinded, or determined by judicial or other authority to be invalid for any reason. (Pub.L. 90-321, Title VIII, Sec. 813, as added Pub.L. 95- 109, Sept. 20, 1977, 91 Stat. 881.)

CHAPTER 16

THE TRUTH IN LENDING ACT

Summary

The Truth in Lending Act (TLA), 1989, requires creditors to reveal basic information about the cost of buying on credit or taking out a loan.

Truth in Lending requires that creditors tell you the actual cost of the credit plan, including interest rate or finance charge and annual percentage rate (APR). This information must be disclosed in writing and must be stated in language that is easily understood.

Specifically, the following information must be disclosed:

- Which method of calculating balances is used:

    1. Average daily balance, with and without new charges
    2. 2-cycle average daily balance, with and without new charges
    3. Previous balance

4.   Adjusted balance

- Annual percentage rate (APR)

- Monthly finance charge; average daily periodic rate

- Late payment penalties

- Due date

- Total amount that will be paid out by the time the loan is paid off

- Any prepayment penalty

- For variable interest rates: when it might change, how this is determined, and within what limits it might change. The consumer must also be notified of any such changes.

- How many payments are to be made.

- A description of any property used as collateral to secure credit on a loan and under what circumstances it might have to be forfeited.

- Creditors must give at least a two-week "grace period" for payments to be made in order to avoid interest payments.

- Any different interest rates within the same credit plan (for cash advances, etc.).

If a creditor is suspected of violating the TLA, you may sue for actual damages and, in some cases twice the finance charges in some cases. The court may award from $100-$1,000 in damages, plus court costs and attorney fees, if you win the suit. You may also file a class action suit.

THE TRUTH IN LENDING ACT

CONSUMER CREDIT PROTECTION ACT

Public Law 90-321; 82 Stat. 146

An Act to safeguard the consumer in connection with the utilization of credit by requiring full disclosure of the terms and conditions of finance charges in credit transactions or in offers to extend credit; by restricting the garnishment of wages; and by creating the National Commission on Consumer Finance to study and make recommendations on the need for further regulation of the consumer finance industry; and for other purposes.

"Be it enacted by the Senate and House of Representatives of the United States of America in Congress assembled, That:

Sec. 1. Short title of entire Act
This Act may be cited as the Consumer Credit Protection Act.

TITLE 1 - **CONSUMER CREDIT COST DISCLOSURE**

Chapter

Chapter 1 - **General Provisions**

Sec. 101. **Short title**

This title may be cited as the Truth in Lending Act.

Sec. 102. **Findings and declaration of purpose**

The Congress finds that economic stabilization would be enhanced and the competition among the various financial institutions and other firms engaged in the extension of consumer credit would be strengthened by the informed use of credit. The informed use of credit results from an awareness of the cost thereof by consumers. It is the purpose of the title to assure a meaningful disclosure of credit terms so that the consumer will be able to compare more readily the various credit terms available to him and avoid the uninformed use of credit.

Sec. 103. **Definitions and rules of construction**

(a) The definitions and rules of construction set forth in this section are applicable for the purposes of this title.

(b) The term 'Board' refers to the Board of Governors of the Federal Reserve System.

c) The term 'organization' means a corporation, government or governmental subdivision or agency, trust, estate, partnership, cooperative, or association.

(d) The term 'person' means a natural person or an organization.

(e) The term 'credit' means the right granted by a creditor to a debtor to defer payment of debt or to incur debt and defer its payment.

(f) The term 'creditor' refers only to creditors who regularly extend, or arrange for the extension of, credit for which the payment of a finance charge is required, whether in connection with loans, sales of property or services, or otherwise. The provisions of this title apply to any such creditor, irrespective of his or its status as a natural person or any type of organization.

(g) The term 'credit sale' refers to any sale with respect to which credit is extended or arranged by the seller. The term includes any contract in the form of a bailment or lease if the bailee or lessee contracts to pay as compensation for use a sum substantially equivalent to or in excess of the aggregate value of the property and services involved and it is agreed that the bailee or lessee will become, or for no other or a nominal consideration has the option to become, the owner of the property upon full compliance with his obligations under the contract.

(h) The adjective 'consumer', used with reference to a credit transaction, characterizes the transaction as one in which the party to whom credit if offered or extended is a natural person, and the money, property, or services which are the subject of the transaction are primarily for personal, family, household, or agricultural purposes.

(I) The term 'open end credit plan' refers to a plan prescribing the terms of credit transactions which may be made thereunder from time to time and under the terms of which a finance charge may be computed on the outstanding unpaid balance from time to time thereunder.

(j) The term 'State' refers to any State, the Commonwealth of Puerto Rico, the District of Columbia, and any territory or possession of the United States.

(k) Any reference to any requirement imposed under this title or any provision thereof includes reference to the regulations of the Board under this title or the provision thereof in question.

(l) The disclosure of an amount or percentage which is greater than the amount or percentage required to be disclosed under this title does not in itself constitute a violation of this title.

> **The first thing that a creditor does is to compare the information on your credit application to the information on your credit report. Any inconsistency might result in immediate rejection.**

Sec. 104. **Exempted transactions**

This title does not apply to the following:
(1) Credit transactions involving extensions of credit for business or commercial purposes, or to government organizations or governmental agencies or instrumentalities, or to
(2) Transactions in securities or commodities accounts by a broker-dealer registered with the Securities and Exchange Commission.
(3) Credit transactions, other than real property transactions, in which the total amount to be financed exceeds $25,000.
(4) Transactions under public utility tariffs, if the Board determines that a State regulatory body regulates the charges for the public utility services involved, the charges for delayed payment, and any discount allowed for early payment.

Sec. 105. **Regulations**

The Board shall prescribe regulations to carry out the purposes of this title. These regulations may contain such classifications, differentiations, or other provisions, and may provide for such adjustments and exceptions for any class of transactions, as in the judgment of the Board are necessary or proper to effectuate the purposes of this title, to prevent circumvention or evasion thereof, or to facilitate compliance therewith.

Sec. 106. **Determination of finance charge**

(a) Except as otherwise provided in this section, the amount of the finance charge in connection with any consumer credit transaction shall be determined as the sum of all charges, payable directly or indirectly by the person to whom the credit is extended, and imposed directly or indirectly by the creditor as an incident to the extension of credit, including any of the following types of charges which are applicable:

(1) Interest, time price differential, and any amount payable under a point, discount, or other system of additional charges.

(2) Service or carrying charge.

(3) Loan fee, finder's fee, or similar charge.

(4) Fee for an investigation or credit report.

(5) Premium or other charge for any guarantee or insurance protecting the creditor against the obligor's default or other credit loss.

(b) Charges or premiums for credit life, accident, or health insurance written in connection with any consumer credit transaction shall be included in the finance charge unless

(1) the coverage of the debtor by the insurance is not a factor in the approval by the creditor of the extension of credit, and this fact is clearly disclosed in writing to the person applying for or obtaining the extension of credit; and

(2) in order to obtain the insurance in connection with the extension of credit, the person to whom the credit is extended must give specific affirmative written indication of his desire to do so after written disclosure to him of the cost thereof.

c) Charges or premiums for insurance, written in connection with any consumer credit transactions, against loss of or damage to property or against liability arising out of the ownership or use of property, shall be included in the finance charge unless a clear and specific statement in writing is furnished by the creditor to the person to whom the credit is extended, setting forth the cost of the insurance if obtained from or through the creditor, and stating that the person to whom the credit is extended may choose the person through which the insurance is to be obtained.

(d) If any of the following items is itemized and disclosed in accordance with the regulations of the Board in connection with any transaction, then the creditor need not include that item in the computation of the finance charge with respect to that transaction:

(1) Fees and charges prescribed by law which actually are or will be paid to public officials for determining the existence of or for perfecting or releasing or satisfying any security related to the credit transactions.

(2) The premium payable for an insurance in lieu of perfecting any security interest otherwise required by the creditor in connection with the transaction, if the premium does not exceed the fees and charges described in paragraph (1) which would otherwise be payable.

(3) Taxes.

(4) Any other type of charge which is not for credit and the exclusion of which from the finance charge is approved by the Board by regulation.

The following items, when charged in connection with any extension of credit secured by an interest in real property, shall not be included in the computation of the finance charge with respect to that transaction:

(1) Fees or premiums for title examination, title insurance, or similar purposes.

(2) Fees for preparation of a deed, settlement statement, or other documents.

(3) Escrows for future payments of taxes and insurance.

(4) Fees for notarizing deeds and other documents.

(5) Appraisal fees.

(6) Credit reports.

Sec. 107. **Determination of annual percentage rate**

(a) The annual percentage rate applicable to any extension of consumer credit shall be determined, in accordance with the regulations of the Board, (1) in the case of any extension of credit other than under an open end credit plan, as

(A) that nominal annual percentage rate which will yield a sum equal to the amount of the finance charge when it is applied to the unpaid balances of the amount financed, calculated according to the actuarial method of allocating payments made on a debt between the amount financed and the amount of the finance charge, pursuant to which a payment is applied first to the accumulated finance charge and the balance is applied to the unpaid amount financed; or

(B) the rate determined by any method prescribed by the Board as a method which materially simplifies computation while retaining reasonable accuracy as compared with the rate determined under subparagraph (A).

(2) in the case of any extension of credit under an open end credit plan, as the quotient (expressed as a percentage) of the total finance charge for the period to which it relates divided by the amount upon which the finance charge for that period is based, multiplied by the number of such periods in a year.

(b) Where a creditor imposes the same finance charge for balances within a specified range, the annual percentage rate shall be computed on the median balance within the range, except that if the Board determines that a rate so computed would not be meaningful, or would be materially misleading, the annual percentage rate shall be computed on such other basis as the Board may be regulation required.

c) The annual percentage rate may be rounded to the nearest quarter of 1 percent for credit transactions payable in substantially equal installments when a creditor determines the total finance charge on the basis of a single add-on, discount, periodic, or other rate, and the rate is converted into an annual percentage rate under procedures prescribed by the Board.

(d) The Board may authorize the use of rate tables or charts which may provide for the disclosure of annual percentage rates which vary from the rate determined in accordance with subsection (a)(1)(A) by not more than such tolerances as the Board may allow. The Board

184

may not allow a tolerance greater than 8 percent of that rate except to simplify compliance where irregular payments are involved.

(e) In the case of creditors determining the annual percentage rate in a manner other than as described in subsection c) or (d), the Board may authorize other reasonable tolerances.

(f) Prior to January 1, 1971, any rate required under this title to be disclosed as a percentage rate may, at the option of the creditor, be expressed in the form of the corresponding ratio of dollars per hundred dollars.

Sec. 108. **Administrative enforcement**

(a) Compliance with the requirements imposed under this title shall be enforced under

(1) section 8 of the Federal Deposit Insurance Act, in the case of

(A) national banks, by the Comptroller of the Currency.

(B) member banks of the Federal Reserve System (other than national banks), by the Board.

(C)banks insured by the Federal Deposit Insurance Corporation (other than members of the Federal Reserve System), by the Board of Directors of the Federal Deposit Insurance Corporation.

(2) section 5(d) of the Home Owners' Loan Act of 1933, section 407 of the National Housing Act, and sections 6(f) and 17 of the Federal Home Bank Act, by the Federal Home Loan Bank Board (acting directly or through the Federal Savings and Loan Insurance Corporation), in the case of any institution subject to any of those provisions.

(3) the Federal Credit Union Act, by the Director of the Bureau of Federal Credit Unions with respect to any Federal credit union.

(4) the Acts to regulate commerce, by the Interstate Commerce Commission with respect to any common carrier subject to those Acts.

(5) the Federal Aviation Act of 1958, by the Civil Aeronautics Board with respect to any air carrier or foreign air carrier subject to that Act.

(6) the Packers and Stockyards Act, 1921 (except as provided in section 406 of at Act), by the Secretary of Agriculture with respect to any activities subject to that Act.

(b) For the Purpose of the Exercise by any agency referred to in subsection (a) of its powers under any Act referred to in that subsection, a violation of any requirement imposed under this title shall be deemed to be a violation of any requirement imposed under that Act. In addition to its powers under any provision of law specifically referred to in subsection (a), each of the agencies referred to in that subsection may exercise, for the purpose of enforcing compliance with any requirement imposed under this title, any other authority conferred on it by law.

c) Except to the extent that enforcement of the requirements imposed under this title is specifically committed to some other Government agency under subsection (a), the Federal Trade Commission shall enforce such requirements. For the purpose of the exercise by the Federal Trade Commission of its functions and powers under the Federal Trade Commission Act, a violation of any requirement imposed under that Act. All of the functions and powers of the Federal Trade Commission under the Federal Trade Commission Act are available to the Commission to enforce compliance by any person with the requirements imposed under this title, irrespective of whether that person is engaged in commerce or meets any other jurisdictional tests in the Federal Trade Commission Act.

(d) The authority of the Board to issue regulations under this title does not impair the authority of any other agency designated in this section to make rules respecting its own procedures in enforcing compliance with requirements imposed under this title.

Sec. 109. **Views of other agencies**

In the exercise of its functions under this title, the Board may obtain upon request the views of any other Federal agency which, in the judgment of the Board, exercises regulatory or supervisory functions with respect to any class of creditors subject to this title.

Sec. 110. **Advisory committee**

The Board shall establish an advisory committee to advise and consult with it in the exercise of its functions under this title. In appointing the members of the committee, the Board shall seek to achieve a fair representation of the interests of sellers of merchandise on credit, lenders, and the public. The committee shall meet from time to time at the call of the Board, and members thereof shall be paid transportation expenses and not to exceed $100 per diem.

Sec. 111. **Effect on other laws**

(a) This title does not annul, alter, or affect, or exempt any creditor from complying with, the laws of any State relating to the disclosure of information in connection with credit transactions, except to the extent that those laws are inconsistent with the provisions of this title or regulations thereunder, and then only to the extent of the inconsistency.

(b) This title does not otherwise annul, alter or affect in any manner the meaning, scope or applicability of the laws of any State, including, but not limited to, laws relating to the types, amounts or rates of charges, or any element or elements of charges, permissible under such laws in connection with the extension or use of credit, nor does this title extend the applicability of those laws to any class of persons or transactions to which they would not otherwise apply.

c) In any action or proceeding in any court involving a consumer credit sale, the disclosure of the annual percentage rate as required under this title in connection with that sale may not be received as evidence that the sale was a loan or any type of transaction other than a credit sale.

(d) Except as specified in sections 125 and 130, this title and the regulations issued thereunder do not affect the validity or enforceability of any contract or obligation under State or Federal law.

Sec. 112. **Criminal liability for willful and knowing violation**

Whoever willfully and knowingly

(1) gives false or inaccurate information or fails to provide information which he is required to disclose under the provisions of this title or any regulation issued thereunder,

(2) uses any chart or table authorized by the Board under section 107 in such a manner as to consistently understate the annual percentage rate determined under section 107(a)(1)(A), or

(3) otherwise fails to comply with any requirement imposed under this title, shall be fined not more than $5,000 or imprisoned not more than one year, or both.

Sec. 113. **Penalties inapplicable to governmental agencies**

No civil or criminal penalty provided under this title for any violation thereof may be imposed upon the United States or any agency thereof, or upon any State or political subdivision thereof, or any agency of any State or political subdivision.

Sec. 114. **Reports by Board and Attorney General**

Not later than January 3 of each year after 1969, the Board and the Attorney General shall, respectively, make reports to the Congress concerning the administration of their functions under this title, including such recommendations as the Board and the Attorney General, respectively, deem necessary or appropriate. In addition, each report of the Board shall include its assessment of the extent to which compliance with the requirements imposed under this title is being achieved.

Chapter 2 - Credit Transactions

Sec. 121. General requirement of disclosure

(a) Each creditor shall disclose clearly and conspicuously, in accordance with the regulations of the Board, to each person to whom consumer credit is extended and upon whom a finance charge is or may be imposed, the information required under this chapter.
(b) If there is more than one obligor, a creditor need not furnish a statement of information required under this chapter to more than one of them.

Sec. 122. Form of disclosure; additional information

(a) Regulations of the Board need not require that disclosures pursuant to this chapter be made in the order set forth in this chapter, and may permit the use of terminology different from that employed in this chapter if it conveys substantially the same meaning.
(b) Any creditor may supply additional information or explanations with any disclosures required under this chapter.

Sec. 123. Exemption for State-regulated transactions

The Board shall be regulation exempt from the requirements of this chapter any class of credit transactions within any State if it determined that under the law of that State that class of transactions is subject to requirements substantially similar to those imposed under this chapter, and that there is adequate provision for enforcement.

Sec. 124. **Effect of subsequent occurrence**

If information disclosed in accordance with this chapter is subsequently rendered inaccurate as the result of any act, occurrence, or agreement subsequent to the delivery of the required disclosures, the inaccuracy resulting therefrom does not constitute a violation of this chapter.

Sec. 125. **Right of rescission as to certain transactions**

(a) Except as otherwise provided in this section, in the case of any consumer credit transaction in which a security interest is retained or acquired in any real property which is used or is expected to be used as the residence of the person to whom credit is extended, the obligor shall have the right to rescind the transaction until midnight of the third business day following the consummation of the transaction or the delivery of the disclosures required under this section and all other material disclosures required under this chapter, whichever is later, by notifying the creditor, in accordance with regulations of the Board, to any obligor in a transaction subject to this section the rights of the obligor under this section. The creditor shall also provide, in accordance with regulations of the Board, an adequate opportunity to the obligor to exercise his right to rescind any transaction subject to this section.

(b) When an obligor exercises his right to rescind under subsection (a), he is not liable for any finance or other charge, and any security interest given by the obligor becomes void upon such a rescission. Within ten days after receipt of a notice of rescission, the creditor shall return to the obligor any money or property given as earnest money, down-payment, or otherwise, and shall take any action necessary or appropriate to reflect the termination of any security interest created under the transaction. If the creditor has delivered any property to the obligor, the obligor may retain possession of it. Upon the performance of the creditor's obligations under this section, the obligor shall tender the property to the creditor, except that if return of the property in kind would be impracticable or inequitable, the obligor shall tender its reasonable value. Tender shall be made at the location of the property or at the residence of the obligor, at the option of the obligor. If the creditor does not take possession of the property within ten days after tender by the obligor, ownership of the property vests in the obligor without obligation on his part to pay for it.

c) Notwithstanding any rule of evidence, written acknowledgment of receipt of any disclosures required under this title by a person to whom a statement is required to be given pursuant to this section does nor more than create a rebuttable presumption of delivery thereof.

(d) The Board may, if it finds that such action is necessary in order to permit homeowners to meet bona fide personal financial emergencies, prescribe regulations authorizing the modification or waiver of any rights created under this section to the extent and under the circumstances set forth in those regulations.

(e) This section does not apply to the creation or retention of a first lien against a dwelling to finance the acquisition of that dwelling.

Sec. 126. **Content of periodic statements**

If a creditor transmits periodic statements in connection with any extension of consumer credit other than under an open end consumer credit plan, then each of those statements shall set forth each of the following items:

(1) The annual percentage rate of the total finance charge.

(2) The date by which, or the period (if any) within which payment must be made in order to avoid additional finance charges or other charges.

(3) Such of the items set forth in section 127(b) as the Board may by regulation require as appropriate to the terms and conditions under which the extension of credit in question is made.

Sec. 127. **Open end consumer credit plans**

(a) Before opening any account under an open end consumer credit plan, the creditor shall disclose to the person to whom credit is to be extended each of the following items, to the extent applicable:

(1) The conditions under which a finance charge may be imposed, including the time period, if any, within which any credit extended may be repaid without incurring a finance charge.

(2) The method of determining the balance upon which a finance charge will be imposed.

(3) The method of determining the amount of the finance charge, including any minimum of fixed amount imposed as a finance charge.

(4) Where one or more periodic rates may be used to compute the finance charge, each such rate, the range of balances to which it is applicable, and the corresponding nominal annual percentage rate determined by multiplying the periodic rate by the number of periods in a year.

(5) If the creditor so elects,

(A) The average effective annual percentage rate of return received from accounts under the plan for a representative period of time; or

(B) whenever circumstances are such that the computation of a rate under subparagraphs (A) would not be feasible or practical, or would be misleading or meaningless, a projected rate of return to be received from accounts under the plan.

The Board shall prescribe regulations, consistent with commonly accepted standards for accounting or statistical procedures, to carry out the purposes of this paragraph.

(6) The conditions under which any other charges may be imposed, and the method by which they will be determined.

(7) The conditions under which the creditor may retain or acquire any security interest in any property to secure the payment of any credit extended under the plan, and a description of the interest or interest which may be so retained or acquired.

(b) The creditor of any account under an open end consumer credit plan shall transmit to the obligor, for each billing cycle at the end of which there is an outstanding balance in that account or with respect to which a finance charge is imposed, a statement setting forth each of the following items to the extent applicable:

(1) The outstanding balance in the account at the beginning of the statement period.

(2) The amount and date of each extension of credit during the period, and, if a purchase was involved, a brief identification (unless previously furnished) of the goods or services purchased.

(3) The total amount credited to the account during the period.

(4) The amount of any finance charge added to the account during the period, itemized to show the amounts, if any, due to the application of percentage rates and the amount, if any, imposed as a minimum or fixed charge.

(5) Where one or more periodic rates may be used to compute the finance charge, each such rate, the range of balances to which it is applicable, and, unless the annual percentage rate (determined under section 107 (a)(2)) is required to be disclosed pursuant to paragraph (6), the corresponding nominal annual percentage rate determined by multiplying the periodic rate by the number of periods in a year.

(6) Where the total finance charge exceeds 50 cents for a monthly or longer billing cycle, or the prorata part of 50 cents for a billing cycle shorter than monthly, the total finance charge expressed as an annual

percentage rate (determined under section 107(a)(2)), except that if the finance charge is the sum of two or more products of a rate times a portion of the balance, the creditor may, in lieu of disclosing a single rate for the total charge, disclose each such rate expressed as an annual percentage rate, and the part of the balance to which it is applicable.

(7) At the election of the creditor, the average effective annual percentage rate of return (or the projected rate) under the plan as prescribed in subsection (a)(5).

(8) The balance on which the finance charge was computed and a statement of how the balance was determined. If the balance is determined without first deducting all credits during the period, that fact and the amount of such payments shall also be disclosed.

(9) The outstanding balance in the account at the end of the period.

(10) The date by which, or the period (if any) within which, payment must be made to avoid additional finance charges.

c) In the case of any open end consumer credit plan in existence on the effective date of this subsection, the items described in subsection (a), to the extent applicable, shall be disclosed in a notice mailed or delivered to the obligor not later than thirty days after that date.

Sec. 128. **Sales not under open end credit plans**

(a) In connection with each consumer credit sale not under an open end credit plan, the creditor shall disclose each of the following items which is applicable:

(1) The case price of the property or service purchased.

(2) The sum of any amounts credited as down payment (including any trade- in).

(3) The difference between the amount referred to in paragraph (1) and the amount referred to in paragraph (2).

(4) All other charges, individually itemized, which are included in the

194

amount of the credit extended but which are not part of the finance charge.

(5) The total amount to be financed (the sum of the amount described in paragraph (3) plus the amount described in paragraph (4)).

(6) Except in the case of a sale of a dwelling, the amount of the finance charge, which may in whole or in part be designated as a time-price differential or any similar term to the extent applicable.

(7) The finance charge expressed as an annual percentage rate except in the case of a finance charge.

(A) which does not exceed $5 and is applicable to an amount financed not exceeding $75, or

(B) which does not exceed $7.50 and is applicable to an amount financed exceeding $75.

A creditor may not divide a consumer credit sale into two or more sales to avoid the disclosure of an annual percentage rate pursuant to this paragraph.

(8) The number, amount, and due dates or periods of payments scheduled to repay the indebtedness.

(9) The default, delinquency, or similar charges payable in the event of late payments.

(10) A description of any security interest held or to be retained or identification of the property to which the security interest relates.

(b) Except as otherwise provided in this chapter, the disclosures required, under subsection (a) shall be made before the credit is extended, and may be made by disclosing the information in the contract or other evidence of indebtedness to be signed by the purchaser.

c) If a creditor receives a purchase order by mail or telephone without personal solicitation, and the cash price and the deferred payment price and the terms of financing, including the annual percentage rate, are set forth in the creditor's catalog or other printed material distributed to the public, then the disclosures required under the first payment is due.

(d) If a consumer credit sale is one of a series of consumer credit sales transactions made pursuant to an agreement providing for the addition of the deferred payment price of that sale to an existing outstanding balance, and the person to whom the credit is extended has approved in writing both the annual percentage rate or rates and the method of computing the finance charge or charges, and the creditor retains no security interest in any property as to which he has received payments aggregating the amount of the sales price including any finance charges attributable thereto, then the disclosure required under subsection(a) for the particular sale may be made at any time not later than the date the first payment for that sale is due. For the purposes of this subsection, in the case of items purchased on different dates, the first purchased shall be deemed first paid for, and in the case of items purchased on the same date, the lowest priced shall be deemed first paid for.

Sec. 129. **Consumer loans not under open end credit plans**

(a) Any creditor making a consumer loan or otherwise extending consumer credit in a transaction which is neither a consumer credit sale nor under an open end consumer credit plan shall disclose each of the following items, to the extent applicable:

(1) The amount of credit of which the obligor will have the actual use, or which is or will be paid to him or for his account or to another person on his behalf.

(2) All charges, individually itemized, which are included in the amount of credit extended but which are not part of the finance charge.

(3) The total amount to be financed (the sum of the amounts referred to in paragraph (1) plus the amounts referred to in paragraph (2)).

(4) Except in the case of a loan secured by a first lien on a dwelling and made to finance the purchase of that dwelling, the amount of the

finance charge.

(5) The finance charge expressed as an annual percentage rate except in the case of a finance charge.

(A) which does not exceed $5 and is applicable to an extension of consumer credit not exceeding $75, or

(B) which does not exceed $7.50 and is applicable to an extension of consumer credit exceeding $75.

A creditor may not divide an extension of credit into two or more transactions to avoid the disclosure of an annual percentage rate pursuant to this paragraph.

(6) The number, amount, and the due dates or periods of payments scheduled to repay the indebtedness.

(7) The default, delinquency, or similar charges payable in the event of late payments.

(8) A description of any security interest held or to be retained or acquired by the creditor in connection with the extension of credit, and a clear identification of the property to which the security interest relates.

(b) Except as otherwise provided in this chapter, the disclosures required by subsection (a) shall be made before the credit is extended, and may be made by disclosing the information in the note or other evidence of indebtedness to be signed by the obligor.

c) If a creditor receives a request for an extension of credit by mail or telephone without personal solicitation and the terms of financing, including the annual percentage rate for representative amounts of credit, are set forth in the creditor's printed material distributed to the public, or in the contract of loan or other printed material delivered to the obligor, then the disclosures required under subsection (a) may be made at any time not later than the date the first payment is due.

Sec. 130. **Civil liability**

(a) Except as otherwise provided in this section, any creditor who fails in connection with any consumer credit transaction to disclose to any person any information required under this chapter to be disclosed to that person is liable to that person in an amount equal to the sum of

(1) twice the amount of the finance charge in connection with the transaction, except that the liability under this paragraph shall not be less than $100 nor greater than $1,000; and

(2) in the case of any successful action to enforce the foregoing liability, the costs of the action together with a reasonable attorney's fee as determined by the court.

(b) A creditor has no liability under this section if within fifteen days after discovering an error, and prior to the institution of an action under this section or the receipt of written notice of the error, the creditor notifies the person concerned of the error and makes whatever adjustments in the appropriate account are necessary to insure that the person will not be required to pay a finance charge in excess of the amount or percentage rate actually disclosed.

c) A creditor may not be held liable in any action brought under this section for a violation of this chapter if the creditor shows by a preponderance of evidence that the violation was not intentional and resulted from a bona fide error notwithstanding the maintenance of procedures reasonably adapted to avoid any such error.

(d) Any action which may be brought under this section against the original creditor in any credit transaction involving a security interest in real property may be maintained against any subsequent assignee of the original creditor where the assignee, its subsidiaries, or affiliates were in a continuing business relationship with the original creditor either at the time the credit was extended or at the time of the assignment, unless the assignment was involuntary, or the assignee shows by a preponderance of evidence that it did not have reasonable grounds to believe that the original creditor was engaged in violations of this chapter, and that is maintained procedures reasonably adapted to apprise it of the existence of any such violations.

(e) Any action under this section may be brought in any United States district court, or in any other court of competent jurisdiction within one year from the date of the occurrence of the violation.

Sec. 131. **Written acknowledgment as proof of receipt**

Except as provided in section 125c) and except in the case of actions brought under section 130(d), in any action or proceeding by or against any subsequent assignee of the original creditor without knowledge to the contrary by the assignee when he acquires the obligation, written acknowledgment of receipt by a person to whom a statement is required to be given pursuant to this title shall be conclusive proof of the delivery thereof and, unless the violation is apparent on the face of the delivery thereof and, unless the violation is apparent on the face of the statement, of compliance with this chapter. This section does not affect the rights of the obligor in any action against the original creditor.

Chapter 3 - **Credit Advertising**

Sec. 141. **Catalogs and multiple-page advertisements**

For the purposes of this chapter, a catalog or other multiple-page advertisement shall be considered a single advertisement if it clearly and conspicuously displays a credit terms table on which the information required to be stated under this chapter is clearly set forth.

Sec. 142. **Advertising of down payments and installments**

No advertisement to aid, promote, or assist directly or indirectly any extension of consumer credit may state

(1) that a specific periodic consumer credit amount or installment amount can be arranged, unless the creditor usually and customarily arranges credit payments or installments for that period and in that amount.

(2) that a specified down payment is required in connection with any extension of consumer credit, unless the creditor usually and customarily arranges down payments in that amount.

Sec. 143. **Advertising of open end credit plans**

No advertisement to aid, promote, or assist directly or indirectly the extension of consumer credit under an open end credit plan may set forth any of the specific terms of that plan or the appropriate rate determined under section 127(a)(5) unless it also clearly and conspicuously sets forth all of the following items:

(1) The time period, if any, within which any credit extended may be repaid without incurring a finance charge.

(2) The method of determining the balance upon which a finance charge will be imposed.

(3) The method of determining the amount of the finance charge, including any minimum or fixed amount imposed as a finance charge.

(4) Where periodic rates may be used to compute the finance charge, the periodic rates expressed as annual percentage rates.

(5) Such other or additional information for the advertising of open end credit plans as the Board may by regulation require to provide for adequate comparison of credit costs as between different types of open end credit plans.

Sec. 144. **Advertising of credit other than open end plans**

(a) Except as provided in subsection (b), this section applies to any advertisement to aid, promote, or assist directly or indirectly any consumer credit sale, loan, or other extension of credit subject to the provisoes of this title, other than open end credit plan.

(b) The provisions of this section do not apply to advertisements of residential real estate except to the extent that the Board may by regulation require.

c) If any advertisement to which this section applies states the rate of a finance charge, the advertisement shall state the rate of that charge expressed as an annual percentage rate.

(d) If any advertisement to which this section applies states the amount of the down payment, if any, the amount of any installment payment, the dollar amount of any finance charge, or the number of installments or the period of repayment, then the advertisement shall state all of the following items:

(1) The cash price or the amount of the loan as applicable.

(2) The down payment, if any.

(3) The number, amount, and due dates or period of payments scheduled to repay the indebtedness if the credit is extended.

(4) The rate of the finance charge expressed as an annual percentage rate.

Sec. 145. **Non-liability of media**

There is no liability under this chapter on the part of any owner or personnel, as such, of any medium in which an advertisement appears or through which it is disseminated.

CHAPTER 17

THE FAIR CREDIT REPORTING ACT

Summary

The Fair Credit Reporting Act (FCRA) governs your rights regarding your credit report: what information is contained in it and who can see it. It also allows you to correct inaccurate or erroneous information in your credit report.

- Who can see your credit report: Only those who have legitimate business purposes relating to you; those to whom you are applying for credit; possible employers and insurers.

- The credit bureau must: reveal the information in your credit file upon your request; provide the names of anyone who has seen your file in the past 6 months: help you to understand your credit file.

202

- Upon denial of credit, the credit bureau must send you upon request, free of charge, a copy of your credit report. For a nominal amount, you may obtain a copy of your report whether or not you have been turned down.

- Correcting your credit file: The FCRA allows you to write to the credit bureau and request that any incorrect information be corrected or updated. If the information cannot be verified, it must, by law, be eliminated from the file. Upon your request, this new, corrected information must then be sent to anyone who has seen your file in the last 6 months.

- You are also allowed to add an explanatory statement to your credit file. This statement, limited to 100 words, then becomes part of your credit file and must be shown to anyone requesting your file.

- Any valid negative information will remain on your credit report for 7 years (bankruptcies remain for 10 years). A billing error, properly disputed, may not be reported as a late or withheld payment.

- The consumer may sue a credit bureau for not following the guidelines of the FCRA, and anyone who uses fraud to obtain information about you from your credit file can be fined up to $5,000 or jailed for up to one year.

THE FAIR CREDIT REPORTING ACT

TITLE VI - PROVISIONS RELATING TO CREDIT REPORTING AGENCIES

Amendment of Consumer Credit Protection Act

Sec. 601. **The Consumer Credit Protection Act is amended by adding at the end thereof the following new title:**

Title VI - Consumer Credit Reporting

Sec. 601. **Short title**

This title may be cited as the Fair Credit Reporting Act.

Sec. 602. **Findings and purpose**

(a) The Congress makes the following findings:

(1) The banking system is dependent upon fair and accurate credit reporting. Inaccurate credit reports directly impair the efficiency of the banking system, and unfair credit reporting methods undermine the public confidence which is essential to the continued functioning of the banking system.

(2) An elaborate mechanism has been developed for investigating and evaluating the credit worthiness, credit standing, credit capacity, character, and general reputation of consumers.

(3) Consumer reporting agencies have assumed a vital role in assembling and evaluating consumer credit and other information on consumers.

(4) There is a need to insure that consumer reporting agencies exercise their grave responsibilities with fairness, impartiality and a

respect for the consumer's right to privacy.

(b) It is the purpose of this title to require that consumer reporting agencies adopt reasonable procedures for meeting the needs of commerce for consumer credit, personnel, insurance, and other information in a manner which is fair and equitable to the consumer, with regard to the confidentiality, accuracy, relevancy and proper utilization of such information in accordance with the requirements of this title.

Sec. 603. **Definitions and rules of construction**

(a) Definitions and rules of construction set forth in this section are applicable for the purposes of this title.

(b) The term 'person' means any individual, partnership corporation, trust, estate, cooperative, association, government or governmental sub-division or agency, or other entity.

c) The term 'consumer' means an individual.

(d) The term 'consumer report' means any written, oral, or other communication of any information by a consumer reporting agency bearing on a consumer's credit worthiness, credit standing, credit capacity, character, general reputation, personal characteristics, or mode of living which is used or expected to be used or collected in whole or in part for the purpose of serving as a factor in establishing the consumer's eligibility for (1) credit or insurance to be used primarily for personal, family, or household purposes, or (2) employment purposes, of (3) other purposes authorized under section 604. The term does not include (A) any report containing information solely as to transactions or experiences between the consumer and the person making the report; (B) any authorization or approval of a specific extension of credit directly or indirectly by the issuer of a credit card or similar device; or C) any report in which a person who has been requested by a third party to make a specific extension of credit directly or indirectly to a consumer conveys his decision with respect to such request, if the third party advises the consumer of the name and address of the person to whom the request was made and such person makes the disclosures to the consumer required under section 615.

(e) The term 'investigative consumer report' means a consumer report or portion thereof in which information on a consumer's character, general reputation, personal characteristics, or mode of living is obtained through personal interviews with neighbors, friends, or associates of the consumer reported on or with others with whom he is acquainted or who may have knowledge concerning any such terms of information. However, such information shall not include specific factual information on a consumer's credit record obtained directly from a creditor of the consumer or from a consumer reporting agency when such information was obtained directly from a creditor of the consumer or from the consumer.

(f) The term 'consumer reporting agency' means any person which, for monetary fees, dues, or on a cooperative nonprofit basis, regularly engages in whole or in part in the practice of assembling or evaluating consumer credit information or other information on consumers for the purpose of furnishing consumer reports to third parties, and which uses any means or facility of interstate commerce for the purpose of preparing or furnishing consumer reports.

(g) The term 'file' when used in connection with information on any consumer, means all of the information on that consumer recorded and retained by a consumer reporting agency regardless of how the information is stored.

(h) The term 'employment purposes' when used in connection with a consumer report means a report used for the purpose of evaluating a consumer for employment, promotion, reassignment, or retention as an employee.

(I) The term 'medical information' means information or records obtained, with the consent of the individual to whom it relates, from licensed physicians or medical practitioners, hospitals, clinics, or other medical or medically related facilities.

Sec. 604. **Permissible purposes of reports**

A consumer reporting agency may furnish a consumer report under the following circumstances and no other:

(1) In response to the order of a court having jurisdiction to issue such an order.

(2) In accordance with the written instructions of the consumer to whom it relates.

(3) To a person which it has reason to believe -

(A) intends to use the information in connection with a credit transaction involving the consumer on whom the information is to be furnished and involving the extension of credit to, or review or collection of an account of, the consumer; or

(B) intends to use the information for employment purposes; or

C) intends to use the information in connection with the underwriting of insurance involving the consumer; or

(D) intends to use the information in connection with a determination of the consumer's eligibility for a license or other benefit granted by a governmental instrumentality required by law to consider an applicant's financial responsibility or status; or

(E) otherwise has a legitimate business need for the information in connection with a business transaction involving the consumer.

In 1991, card holders of Visa and MasterCard generated an income revenue of 34 billion dollars from interest rates and annual fees alone.

Sec. 605. **Obsolete information**

(a) Except as authorized under subsection (b), no consumer reporting agency may make any consumer report containing any of the following items of information:

(1) Cases under title 11 of the United States Code or under the Bankruptcy Act that, from the date of entry of the order for relief or the date of adjudication, as the case may be, antedate the report by more than 10 years.

(2) Suits and judgments which, from date of entry, antedate the report by more than seven years or until the governing statute of limitations has expired, whichever is the longer period.

(3) Paid tax liens which, from date of payment, antedate the report by more than seven years.

(4) Accounts placed for collection or charged to profit and loss which antedate the report by more than seven years.

(5) Records of arrest, indictment, or conviction of crime which, from date of disposition, release, or parole, antedate the report by more than seven years.

(6) Any other adverse item of information which antedates the report by more than seven years.

(b) The provisions of subsection (a) are not applicable in the case of any consumer credit report to be used in connection with -

(1) a credit transaction involving, or which may reasonable be expected to involve, a principal amount of $50,000 or more;

(2) the underwriting of life insurance involving, or which may reasonable be expected to involve, a face amount of $50,000 or more; or

(3) the employment of any individual at an annual salary which equals, or which may reasonable be expected to equal $20,000, or more.

Sec. 606. **Disclosure of investigative consumer reports**

(a) A person may not procure or cause to be prepared an investigative consumer report on any consumer unless -

(1) it is clearly and accurately disclosed to the consumer that an investigative consumer report including information as to his character, general reputation, personal characteristics, and mode of living, whichever are applicable, may be made, and such disclosure (A) is made in a writing mailed, or otherwise delivered, to the consumer, not later than three days after the date on which the report was first requested, and (B) includes a statement informing the consumer of his right to request the additional disclosures provided for under subsection (b) of this section; or

(2) the report is to be used for employment purposes for which the consumer has not specifically applied.

(b) Any person who procures or causes to be prepared an investigative consumer report on any consumer shall, upon written request made by the consumer within a reasonable period of time after the receipt by him of the disclosure required by subsection (a) (1), make a complete and accurate disclosure of the nature and scope f the investigation requested. This disclosure shall be made in a writing
mailed, or otherwise delivered, to the consumer not later than five days after the date on which the request for such disclosure was received from the consumer or such report was first requested, whichever is the later.

c) No person may be held liable for any violation of subsection (a) or (b) of this section if he shows by a preponderance of the evidence that at the time of the violation he maintained reasonable procedures to assure compliance with subsection (a) or (b).

Sec. 607. **Compliance procedures**

(a) Every consumer reporting agency shall maintain reasonable procedures designed to avoid violations of section 605 and to limit the furnishing of consumer reports to the purposes listed under section 604. These procedures shall require that prospective users of the information identify themselves, certify the purposes for which the information is sought, and certify that the information will be used for no other purpose. Every consumer reporting agency shall make a reasonable effort to verify the identity of a new prospective user and the uses certified by such prospective user prior to

Only one third of all card holders pay all charges in full within the grace period.

furnishing such user a consumer report. No consumer reporting agency may furnish a consumer report to any person if it has reasonable grounds for believing that the consumer report will not be used for a purpose listed in section 604.

(b) Whenever a consumer reporting agency prepares a consumer report it shall follow reasonable procedures to assure maximum possible accuracy of the information concerning the individual about whom the report related.

Sec. 608. **Disclosures to governmental agencies**

Notwithstanding the provisions of section 604, a consumer reporting agency may furnish identifying information respecting any consumer, limited to his name, address, former addresses, places of employment, or former places of employment, to a governmental agency.

Sec. 609. **Disclosures to consumers**

(a) Every consumer reporting agency shall, upon request and proper identification of any consumer, clearly and accurately disclose to the consumer:

(1) The nature and substance of all information (except medical information) in its files on the consumer at the time of the request.

(2) The sources of the information; except that the sources of information acquired solely for use in preparing an investigative consumer report and actually used for no other purpose need not be disclosed. Provided, That in the event an action is brought under this title, such sources shall be available to the plaintiff under appropriate discovery procedures in the court in which the action is brought.

(3) The recipients of any consumer report on the consumer which it has furnished-

(A) for employment purposes within the two-year period preceding the request, and

(B) for any other purpose within the six-month period preceding the request.

(b) The requirements of subsection (a) respecting the disclosure of sources of information and the recipients of consumer reports do not apply to information received or consumer reports furnished prior to the effective date of this title except to the extent that the matter involved is contained in the files of the consumer reporting agency on that date.

Sec. 610. **Conditions of disclosure to consumers**

(a) A consumer reporting agency shall make the disclosures required under section 609 during normal business hours and on reasonable notice.

(b) The disclosures required under section 609 shall be made to the consumer -

(1) in person if he appears in person and furnishes proper identification; or

(2) by telephone if he has made a written request, with proper identification, for telephone disclosure and the toll charge, if any, for the telephone call is prepaid by or charged directly to the consumer.

c) Any consumer reporting agency shall provide trained personnel to explain to the consumer any information furnished to him pursuant to section 609.

(d) The consumer shall be permitted to be accompanied by one other person of his choosing, who shall furnish reasonable identification. A consumer reporting agency may require the consumer to furnish a written statement granting permission to the consumer reporting agency to discuss the consumer's file in such person's presence.

(e) Except as provided in sections 616 and 617, no consumer may bring any action or proceeding in the nature of defamation, invasion of privacy, or negligence with respect to the reporting of information against any consumer reporting agency, any user of information, or any person who furnishes information to a consumer reporting agency, based on information disclosed pursuant to section 609, 610, or 615, except as to false information furnished with malice or willful intent to injure such consumer.

Sec. 611. **Procedure in case of disputed accuracy**

(a) If the completeness or accuracy of any item of information contained in his file is disputed by a consumer, and such dispute is directly conveyed to the consumer reporting agency by the consumer, the consumer reporting agency shall within a reasonable period of time reinvestigate and record the current status of that information unless it has reasonable grounds to believe that the dispute by the consumer is frivolous or irrelevant. If after such reinvestigation such information is found to be inaccurate or can no longer be verified, the consumer reporting agency shall promptly delete such information. The presence of contradictory information in the consumer's file does not in and of itself constitute reasonable grounds for believing the dispute is frivolous or irrelevant.

(b) If the reinvestigation does not resolve the dispute, the consumer may file a brief statement setting forth the nature of the dispute. The consumer reporting agency may limit such statements to not more than one hundred words if it provides the consumer with assistance in writing a clear summary of the dispute.

c) Whenever a statement of a dispute is filed, unless there is reasonable grounds to believe that it is frivolous or irrelevant, the consumer reporting agency shall, in any subsequent consumer report containing the information in question, clearly note that it is disputed by the consumer and provide either the consumer's statement or a clear and accurate codification or summary thereof.

(d) Following any deletion of information which is found to be inaccurate or whose accuracy can no longer be verified or any notation as to disputed information, the consumer reporting agency shall, at the request of the consumer, furnish notification that the item has been deleted or the statement, codification, or summary pursuant to subsection (b) or c) to any person specifically designated by the consumer who has within two years prior thereto received a consumer report for employment purposes, or within six months prior thereto received a consumer report for any other purpose, which contained the deleted or disputed information. The consumer reporting agency shall clearly and conspicuously disclose to the consumer his rights to make such a request. Such disclosure shall be made at or prior to the time the information is deleted or the consumer's statement regarding the disputed information is received.

Sec. 612. **Charges for certain disclosures**

A consumer reporting agency shall make all disclosure pursuant to section 609 and furnish all consumer reports pursuant to section 611 (d) without charge to the consumer if, within thirty days after receipt by such consumer of a notification pursuant to section 615 or notification from"Sec. 612. a debt collection agency affiliated with such consumer reporting agency stating that the consumer's credit rating may be or has been adversely affected, the consumer makes a request under section 609 or 611 (d). Otherwise, the consumer reporting agency may impose a reasonable charge on the consumer for making disclosure to such consumer pursuant to section 609, the charge for which shall be indicated to the consumer prior to making disclosure; and for furnishing notifications, statements, summaries, or codifications to person designated by the consumer pursuant to section 611 (d), the charge for which shall be indicated to the consumer prior to furnishing such information, and shall not exceed the charge that the consumer reporting agency would impose on each designated recipient for a consumer report except that no charge may be made for notifying such persons of the deletion of information which is found to be inaccurate or which can no longer be verified.

Sec. 613. **Public record information for employment purposes**

A consumer reporting agency which furnishes a consumer report for employment purposes and which for that purpose compiles and reports items of information on consumers which are matters of public record and are likely to have an adverse effect upon a consumer's ability to obtain employment shall -

(1) at the time such public record information is reported to the user of such consumer report, notify the consumer of the fact that public record information is being reported by the consumer reporting agency, together with the name and address of the person to whom such information is being reported; or

(2) maintain strict procedures designed to insure that whenever public record information which is likely to have an adverse effect on a consumer's ability to obtain employment is reported it is complete and up to date. For purposes of this paragraph, items of public record relating to arrest, indictments, convictions, suits, tax liens, and outstanding judgments shall be considered up to date if the current public record status of the item at the time of the report is reported.

Sec. 614. **Restrictions on investigative consumer reports**

Whenever a consumer reporting agency prepares an investigative consumer report, no adverse information in the consumer report (other than information which is a matter of public record) may be included in a subsequent consumer report unless such adverse information has been verified in the process of making such subsequent consumer report, or the adverse information was received within the three-month period preceding the date the subsequent report is furnished.

Sec. 615. **Requirements on users of consumer reports**

(a) Whenever credit or insurance for personal, family, or household purposes, or employment involving a consumer is denied or the charge for such credit or insurance is increased either wholly or partly because of information contained in a consumer report from a consumer reporting agency, the user of the consumer report shall so advise the consumer against whom such adverse action has been taken and supply the name and address of the consumer reporting agency making the report.

(b) Whenever credit for personal, family, or household purposes involving a consumer is denied or the charge for such credit is increased either wholly or partly because of information obtained from a person other than a consumer reporting agency bearing upon the consumer's credit worthiness, credit standing, credit capacity, character, general reputation, personal characteristics, or mode of living, the user of such information shall, within a reasonable period of time, upon the consumer's written request for the reasons for such adverse action received within sixty days after learning of such adverse action, disclose the nature of the information to the consumer. The user of such information shall clearly and accurately disclose to the consumer his right to make such written requests at the time such adverse action is communicated to the consumer.

c) No person shall be held liable for any violation of this section if he shows by a preponderance of the evidence that at the time of the alleged violation he maintained reasonable procedures to assure compliance with the provisions of subsections (a) and (b).

Sec. 616. **Civil liability for willful noncompliance**

Any consumer reporting agency or user of information which willfully fails to comply with any requirement imposed under this title with respect to any consumer is liable to that consumer in an amount equal to the sum of -

(1) any actual damages sustained by the consumer as a result of the failure;

(2) such amount of punitive damages as the court may allow, and

(3) in the case of any successful action to enforce any liability under

this section, the costs of the action together with reasonable attorney's fees as determined by the court.

Sec. 617. **Civil liability for negligent noncompliance**

Any consumer reporting agency or user of information which is negligent in failing to comply with any requirement imposed under this title with respect to any consumer is liable to that consumer in an amount equal to the sum of -
(1) any actual damages sustained by the consumer as a result of the failure;
(2) in the case of any successful action to enforce any liability under this section, the costs of the action together with reasonable attorney's fees as determined by the court.

Sec. 618. **Jurisdiction of courts; limitation of actions**

An action to enforce any liability created under this title may be brought in any appropriate United States district court without regard to the amount in controversy, or in any other court of competent jurisdiction, within two years from the date on which the liability arises, except that where a defendant has materially and willfully misrepresented any information required under this title to be disclosed to an individual and the information so misrepresented is material to the establishment of the defendant's liability to that individual under this title, the action may be brought at any time within two years after discovery by the individual of the misrepresentation.

Sec. 619. **Obtaining information under false pretenses**

Any person who knowingly and willfully obtains information on a consumer from a consumer reporting agency under false pretense shall be fined not more than $5,000 or imprisoned not more than one year, or both.

Sec. 620. **Unauthorized disclosures by officers or employees**

Any officer or employee of a consumer reporting agency who knowingly and willfully provides information concerning an individual from the agency's files to a person not authorized to receive that information shall be fined not more than $5,000 or imprisoned not more than one year, or both.

CHAPTER 18

THE FAIR
CREDIT BILLING
ACT

Summary

The Fair Credit Billing Act (FCBA) is designed to protect the consumer from unauthorized charges or mistakes on the credit card billing statement.

- FCBA enables the consumer to dispute billing mistakes on the credit card statement. Mistakes include:

  ▸ Computational errors
  ▸ Failure to post credit for a payment
  ▸ Failure to send a statement
  ▸ Unauthorized charges
  ▸ Unrecognizable charges
  ▸ Charges for goods not received, not delivered, or not accepted
  ▸ Charges for goods that were delivered but were other than what was ordered.

- If a violation occurs or is suspected, the consumer must write the creditor within 60 days of the first bill. This correspondence must be acknowledged within 30 days, and you must be notified within 90 days-- with proof-- that the problem has been corrected or that the bill is correct. In your correspondence, the following must be stated:

  - That you believe the billing to be in error, why, and the amount of money involved.

  - Your name and account number.

- While the dispute is in process, you may withhold payment for the disputed charge (not for any other charges on the bill), including finance charges. The creditor may not take any legal action against you until the dispute has been settled.

THE FAIR CREDIT BILLING ACT

Title III - Fair Credit Billing

Sec. 301. **Short Title**

This title may be cited as the "Fair Credit Billing Act."

Sec. 302. **Declaration of purpose**

The last sentence of section 102 of the Truth in Lending Act (15 U.S.C. 1601) is amended by striking out the period and inserting in lieu thereof a comma and the following: and to protect the consumer against inaccurate and unfair credit billing and credit card practices.

Sec. 202. **Definitions of creditor and open end credit plan**

The first sentence of section 103 (f) of the Truth in Lending Act (15 U.S.C. 1602 (f) is amended to read as follows: "The term 'creditor' refers only to creditors who regularly extend, or arrange for the extension of, credit which is payable by agreement in more than four installments or for which the payment of a finance charge is or may be required, whether in connection with loans, sales of property or services, or otherwise. For the purposes of the requirements imposed under Chapter 4 and sections 127 (a)(6), 127(a)(7), 127(a)(8), 127(b)(1), 127(b)(2), 127(b)(3), 127(b)(9), and 127(b)(11) of Chapter 2 of this Title, the term 'creditor' shall also include card issuers whether or not the amount due is payable by agreement in more than four installments or the payment of a finance charge is or may be required, and the Board shall, by regulation, apply these requirements to such card issuers, to the extent appropriate, even though the requirements are by their terms applicable only to creditors offering open end credit plans.

Sec. 304. **Disclosure of fair credit billing right**

(a) Section 127 (a) of the Truth in Lending Act (15 U.S.C. 1637 (a) is amended by adding at the end thereof a new paragraph as follows: "(8) A statement in a form prescribed by regulations of the Board of the protection provided by sections 161 and 170 to an obligor and the creditor's responsibilities under sections 162 and 170. With respect to each of two billing cycles per year, at semiannual intervals, the creditor shall transmit such statement to each obligor to whom the creditor is required to transmit a statement pursuant to section 127(b) for such billing cycle."
"(b) Section 127c) of such Act (15 U.S.C. 1637 c) is amended to read:
"(c) In the case of any existing account under an open end consumer credit plan having an outstanding balance of more than $1 at or after the close of the creditor's first full billing cycle under the plan after the effective date of subsection (a) or any amendments thereto, the items described in subsection (a), to the extent applicable and not previously disclosed, shall be disclosed in a notice mailed or delivered to the obligor not later than the time of mailing the next statement required by subsections (b)."

Sec. 305. **Disclosure of billing contact**

Section 127 (b) of the Truth in Lending Act (15 U.S.C. 1637 (b) is amended by adding at the end thereof a new paragraph as follows: "(11) The address to be used by the creditor for the purpose of receiving billing inquiries from the obligor."

Sec. 306. **Billing practices**

The Truth in Lending Act (15 U.S.C. 1601-1665) is amended by
adding at the end thereof a new chapter as follows:

Chapter 4 - **Credit Billing**

Sec. 161. **Correction of billing errors:**

(a) If a creditor, within sixty days after having transmitted to an
obligor a statement of the obligor's account in connection with an
extension of consumer credit, receives at the address disclosed under
section 127(b)(11) a written notice (other than notice on a payment
stub or other payment medium supplied by the creditor if the creditor
so stipulates with the disclosure required under section 127(a)(8))
from the obligor in which the obligor -
(1) sets forth or otherwise enables the creditor to identify the name
and account number (if any) of the obligor.
(2) indicates the obligor's belief that the statement contains a billing
error and the amount of such billing error, and
(3) sets forth the reasons for the obligor's belief (to the extent
applicable) that the statement contains a billing error, the creditor
shall, unless the obligor has, after giving such written notice and
before the expiration of the time limits herein specified, agreed that
the statement was correct -
(A) not later than thirty days after the receipt of the notice, send a
written acknowledgment thereof to the obligor, unless the action
required in subparagraph (B) is taken within such thirty-day period,
and
(B) not later than two complete billing cycles of the creditor (in no
event later than ninety days) after the receipt of the notice and prior
to taking any action to collect the amount, or any part thereof,

indicated by the obligor under paragraph (2) either -

(I) make appropriate corrections in the account of this obligor, including the crediting of any finance charges on amounts erroneously billed, and transmit to the obligor a notification of such corrections and the creditor's explanation of any change in the amount indicated by the obligor under paragraph (2) and, if any such change is made and the obligor so requests, copies of documentary evidence of the obligor's indebtedness; or

(ii) send a written explanation or clarification to the obligor, after having conducted an investigation, setting forth to the extent applicable the reasons why the creditor believes the account of the obligor was correctly shown in the statement and, upon request of the obligor, provide copies of documentary evidence of the obligor's indebtedness. In the case of a billing error where no obligor alleges that the creditor's billing statement reflects goods not delivered to the obligor or his designee in accordance with the agreement made at the time of the transaction, a creditor may not construe such amount to be correctly shown unless he determines that such goods were actually delivered, mailed, or otherwise sent to the obligor and provides the obligor with a statement of such determination.

After complying with the provisions of this subsection with respect to an alleged billing error, a creditor has no further responsibility under this section if the obligor continues to make substantially the same allegation with respect to such error.

(b) For the purpose of this section, a 'billing error' consists of any of the following:

(1) A reflection on a statement of an extension of credit which was not made to the obligor or, if made, was not in the amount reflected on such statement.

(2) A reflection on a statement of an extension of credit for which the obligor requests additional clarification including documentary

evidence thereof.

(3) A reflection on a statement of goods or services not accepted by the obligor or his designee or not delivered to the obligor or his designee in accordance with the agreement made at the time of a transaction.

(4) The creditor's failure to reflect properly on a statement a payment made by the obligor or a credit issued to the obligor.

(5) A computation error or similar error of an accounting nature of the creditor on a statement.

(6) Any other error described in regulations of the Board.

c) For the purposes of this section, 'action to collect the amount', or any part thereof, indicated by an obligor under paragraph (2) does not include the sending of statements of account to the obligor following written notice from the obligor as specified under subsection (a), if -

(1) the obligor's account is not restricted or closed because of the failure of the obligor to pay the amount indicated under paragraph (2) of subsection (a), and

(2) the creditor indicates the payment of such amount is not required pending the creditor's compliance with this section.

Nothing in this section shall be construed to prohibit any action by a creditor to collect any amount which has not been indicated by the obligor to contain a billing error.

(d) Pursuant to regulations of the Board, a creditor operating an open end consumer credit plan may not, prior to the sending of the written explanation or clarification required under paragraph (B) (ii), restrict or close an account with respect to which the obligor has indicated pursuant to subsection (a) that he believes such account to contain a billing error solely because of the obligor's failure to pay the amount indicated to be in error.

Nothing in this subsection shall be deemed to prohibit a creditor from applying against the credit limit on the obligor's account the amount indicated to be in error.

(e) Any creditor who fails to comply with the requirements of this section or section 162 forfeits any right to collect from the obligor the amount indicated by the obligor under paragraph (2) of subsection (a) of this section, and any finance charges thereon, except that the amount required to be forfeited under this subsection may not exceed $50.

> **If the creditor does not respond to the investigation of the credit bureau within a "reasonable time," for any reason, the credit bureau must erase the entry. "Reasonable time" is interpreted by the courts as 30 days.**

Sec. 162. **Regulation of credit reports**

(a) After receiving a notice from an obligor as provided in section 161(a), a creditor or his agent may not directly or indirectly threaten to report to any person adversely on the obligor's credit rating or credit standing because of the obligor's failure to pay the amount indicated by the obligor under section 161(a)(2), and such amount may not be reported as delinquent to any third party until the creditor has met the requirements of section 161 and has allowed the obligor the same number of days (not less than ten) thereafter to make payment as is provided under the credit agreement with the obligor for the payment of undisputed amounts.

(b) If a creditor receives a further written notice from an obligor that an amount is still in dispute within the time allowed for payment under subsection (a) of this section, a creditor may not report to any third party that the amount of the obligor is delinquent because the obligor has failed to pay an amount which he has indicated under section 171 (a)(2), unless the creditor also reports that the amount is in dispute and, at the same time, notifies the obligor of the name and address of each party to whom the creditor is reporting information concerning the delinquency.

(c)A creditor shall report any subsequent resolution of any delinquencies reported pursuant to subsection (b) to the parties to whom such delinquencies were initially reported.

Sec. 163. **Length of billing period**

(a) If an open end consumer credit plan provides a time period within which an obligor may repay any portion of the credit extended without incurring an additional finance charge, such additional finance charge may not be imposed with respect to such portion of the credit extended for the billing cycle of which such period is a part unless a statement which includes the amount upon which the finance charge for that period is based was mailed at least fourteen days prior to the date specified in the statement by which payment must be made in order to avoid imposition of that finance charge.

(b) Subsection (a) does not apply in any case where a creditor has been presented, delayed, or hindered in making timely mailing or delivery of such periodic statement within the time period specified in such subsection because of an act of God, war, natural disaster, strike, or other excusable or justifiable cause, as determined under regulations of the Board.

Sec. 164. **Prompt crediting of payments**

Payments received from an obligor under an open end consumer credit plan by the creditor shall be posted promptly to the obligor's account as specified in regulations of the Board. Such regulations shall prevent a finance charge from being imposed on any obligor if the creditor has received the obligor's payment in readily identifiable form in the amount, manner, location, and time indicated by the credit to avoid the imposition thereof.

Sec. 165. **Crediting excess payments**

Whenever an obligor transmits funds to a creditor in excess of the total balance due on an open end consumer credit account, the creditor shall promptly (1) upon request of the obligor refund the amount of the overpayment, or (2) credit such amount to the obligor's account.

Sec. 166. **Prompt notification of returns**

With respect to any sales transaction where a credit card has been used to obtain credit, where the seller is a person other than the card issuer, and where the seller accepts or allows a return of the goods or forgiveness of a debt for services which were the subject of such sale, the seller shall promptly transmit to the credit card issuer, a credit statement with respect thereto, and the credit card issuer shall credit the account of the obligor for the amount of the transaction.

Sec. 167. **Use of cash discounts**

(a) With respect to credit cards which may be used for extensions of credit in sales transactions in which the seller is a person other than the card issuer; the card issuer may not, by contract or otherwise, prohibit any such seller from offering a discount to a cardholder to induce the cardholder to pay by cash, check, or similar means rather than use a credit card.

(b) With respect to any sales transaction, any discount not in excess of 5 per centum offered by the seller for the purpose of inducing payment by cash, check, or other means not involving the use of a credit card shall not constitute a finance charge as determined under section 106, if such discount is offered to all prospective buyers and its availability is disclosed to all prospective buyers clearly and conspicuously in accordance with regulations of the Board.

Sec. 168. **Prohibition of tie-in services**

Notwithstanding any agreement to the contrary, a card issuer may not require a seller, as a condition to participating in a credit card plan, to open an account with or procure any other service from the card issuer or its subsidiary or agent.

Sec. 169. **Prohibition of offsets**

(a) A card issuer may not take any action to offset a cardholder's indebtedness arising in connection with a consumer credit transaction under the relevant credit card plan against funds of the cardholder held on deposit with the card issuer unless -
(1) such action was previously authorized in writing by the cardholder in accordance with a credit plan whereby the cardholder agrees periodically to pay debts incurred in his open end credit account by permitting the card issuer periodically to deduct all or a portion of such debt from the cardholder's deposit account, and
(2) such action with respect to any outstanding disputed amount not be taken by the card issuer upon request of the cardholder. In the case of any credit card account in existence on the effective date of this section, the previous written authorization referred to in clause (1) shall not be required until the date (after such effective date) when such account is renewed, but in no case later than one year

after such effective date. Such written authorization shall be deemed
to exist if the card issuer has previously notified the cardholder that
the use of his credit card account will subject any funds which the
card issuer holds in deposit accounts of such cardholder to offset
against any amounts due and payable on his credit card account
which have not been paid in accordance with the terms of the
agreement between the card issuer and the cardholder.

(b) This section does not alter or affect the right under State law of
a card issuer to attach or otherwise levy upon funds of a cardholder
held on deposit with the card issuer if that remedy is constitutionally
available to creditors generally.

Sec. 170. **Rights of credit card customers**

(a) Subject to the limitation contained in subsection (b), a card issuer
who has issued a credit card to a cardholder pursuant to an open end
consumer credit plan shall be subject to all claims (other than tort
claims) and defenses arising out of any transaction in which the credit
card is used as a method of payment or extension of credit if (1) the
obligor has made a good faith attempt to obtain satisfactory
resolution of a disagreement or problem relative to the transaction
from the person honoring the credit card; (2) the amount of the initial
transaction exceeds $50; and (3) the place where the initial
transaction occurred was in the same State as the mailing address
previously provided by the cardholder or was within 100 miles from
such address, except that the limitations set forth in clauses (2) and
(3) with respect to an obligor's right to assert claims and defenses
against a card issuer shall not be applicable to any transaction in
which the person honoring the credit card (A) is the same person as
the card issuer, (B) is controlled by the card issuer, C) is under direct
or indirect common control with the card issuer, (D) is a franchised
dealer in the card issuer's products or services, or (E) has obtained

the order for such transaction through a mail solicitation made by or participated in by the card issuer in which the cardholder is solicited to enter into such transaction by using the credit card issued by the card issuer.

(b) The amount of claims or defenses asserted by the cardholder may not exceed the amount of credit outstanding with respect to such transaction at the time the cardholder first notifies the card issuer or the person honoring the credit card of such claim or defense. For the purpose of determining the amount of credit outstanding in the preceding sentence, payments and credits to the cardholder's account are deemed to have been applied, in the order indicated, to the payment of: (1) late charges in the order of their entry to the account; (2) finance charges in order of their entry to the account; and (3) debits to the account other than those set forth above, in the order in which each debit entry to the account was made.

SECTION FOUR

APPENDICES

APPENDIX 1

A BRIEF HISTORY OF CREDIT

In 1914, a quiet revolution began in the United States. For the first time, consumers could make a purchase using a new-fangled device called a credit card.

This purchasing revolution started on a small scale, with Western Union and a few department stores and oil companies extending credit to their customers. These companies did not recognize each other's cards, and the credit was good only for one month at a time.

By the 1930's, companies were accepting cards other than their own; and by 1950, Diners Club offered a card which was accepted by a wide array of retailers - though the total still had to be paid off in full each month.

Local banks entered the credit card business during the 1950's, offering cards which could be used at many retailers. And consumers could carry over balances from one month to the next.

In the next decade, the Bank of America issued its BankAmericard. Licensed by the Bank of America to other banks, BankAmericard was more widely useful than any previous card. The licensed banks became known as the Visa Association. A similar event created the MasterCard Association.

Why were the Visa and MasterCard Associations so revolutionary? Not only did they enlist millions of merchants nationwide into the credit card system, but they developed a nationwide processing system for credit cards. This was the real beginning of today's credit card industry, with its estimated annual turnover of around $156 billion.

At first a bank was restricted to offering one card; but today most of the 6,000 member banks issue both Visa and MasterCard. Other revolving credit cards include the Discover Card and the American Express Optima Card.

For years, credit card companies were willing to extend credit only to the most credit-worthy consumers. But a case brought before the Supreme Court in 1978 had a major impact on this attitude. The Marquette decision, as it was known, allowed companies to circumvent the usury laws that exist in most states and which limit the percentage of interest a company can charge. The Court said that credit card companies were free to charge the same interest rate nationwide as in their home state. The companies moved their headquarters to the few states without usury laws, and interest rates rose to whatever the market would bear. These higher profits made companies willing to take on more risky clients.

This change resulted in a tremendous demand for credit cards by almost every facet of the population. The fact that a poor credit history seldom bars the way to new credit largely accounts for the growth and expansion of the credit card industry.

A happy revolution, indeed. Except for consumers who have gotten in over their head.

It was for those people that *Second Chance* was written.

APPENDIX 2

HELPFUL ADDRESSES

▸ **American Bankruptcy Institute**
510 C Street N. E.
Washington, D.C.
20002-5810
703-739-0800

This is a non-profit institute for the exchange of information on bankruptcy.

▸ **American Express**
American Express
Tower World
Financial Center
200 Vessey St.
New York, NY 10285
212-640-2000

▸ **Associated Credit Bureaus (ACB)**

1090 Vermont Avenue N.W, #200
Washington, D.C. 20005-4905
202-371-0910

ACB can help you with problems or questions related to credit bureaus

▸ **BankCard Holders of America (BHA)**
560 Herndon Pkwy., Ste. 120
Herndon, VA 22070
800-638-6407

BHA is a non-profit organization for educating

consumers about issues involving credit. They publish a newsletter which is free to BHA members.

> **Better Business Bureau (BBB)**
> **4200 Wilson Boulevard, Ste. 800**
> **Arlington, VA 22203**
> **703-276-0100**

Through its local branches, BBB provides information on businesses such as how long they have been in operation, any complaints against them, etc. Telephone information in your area can give you the local number for your nearest BBB.

> **Board of Governors of the Federal Reserve System Consumer and Community Affairs**
> **20th and C Sts. N.W.**
> **Washington, DC 20551**

For questions regarding state member banks of the federal reserve system.

> **Bureau of Consumer Protection Division of Credit Practices Federal Trade Commission Washington, D.C. 20580**

For questions about other credit card issuers (including retail and gasoline companies).

> **Consumer Credit Card Rating Service**
> **P.O. Box 5483**
> **Oxnard, CA 93031**
> **310-392-7720**

Consumer Credit Card Rating Service offers a listing of over 2,000 low-interest and no-fee Visa and MasterCard credit cards. This list includes standard, gold, secured, and frequent-flyer cards, with their interest rates, annual fees, grace period, and phone number to apply.

They also offers the Credit Card Cost Calculator, a dial which helps you to determine which card is best for you.

▸ **Consumer Credit Counseling Service (CCCS)**
8611 2nd Avenue, Ste 100
Silver Spring, MD 20910
800-388-2227
(National referral line)

Consumer Credit Counseling Service is a free, non-profit service to assist consumers in handling financial problems.

CCCS has hundreds of offices nationwide. The telephone number above will direct you to the CCCS office nearest you.

▸ **Consumer Information Center**
Pueblo, CO 81002
719-948-3334

Consumer Information Center distributes a Consumer Information Catalog listing federal publications dealing with consumer issues. These publications are low-cost or free. The telephone number above will allow you to leave your name and address to receive a copy of the catalog.

▸ **Consumer Protection Offices for the Individual States:**

Alabama
205-242-7334

Arizona
602-542-5763

Arkansas
501-682-2341

California
916-445-1254

Colorado
303-866-4500

Connecticut
203-566-4999

Washington, D.C.
202- 727-7000

Florida
904-488-2226

Georgia
404-651-8600

Hawaii
808-586-2630

Idaho
208-334-2424

Illinois
217-782-0244

Indiana
317-232-6330

Iowa
515-281-5926

Kansas
913-296-3751

Kentucky
502-573-2200

Louisiana
(non-published
number)

Maine
207-624-8527

Maryland
410-528-8662

Massachusetts
617-727-8400

Michigan
517-373-1140

Minnesota
612-296-2331

Mississippi
601-359-4230

Missouri
314-751-3321

Montana
406-444-4312

Nebraska
402-471-2682
Nevada
702-486-7355

New Hampshire
603-271-3641

New Jersey
609-292-4925

New Mexico
505-827-6060

New York
518-474-8583

North Carolina
919-733-7741

North Dakota
701-328-2210

Ohio
614-466-4986

Oklahoma
405-521-4274

Oregon
503-378-4320

Pennsylvania
717-787-9707

Puerto Rico
809-721-0940

Rhode Island
401-277-2104

South Carolina
803-734-3970

South Dakota
605-773-4400

Tennessee
615-741-2672

Texas
512-463-2070

Utah
801-530-6601

Vermont
802-828-3171

Virgin Islands
809-774-3130

Virginia
804-786-2116

Washington
206-753-6210

West Virginia
304-348-8986

Wisconsin
608-224-4949

Wyoming
307-777-7874

▸ **Consumer Reports
Consumers Union
101 Truman Avenue
Yonkers, NY
10703-1057
914-378-2000**

Consumers Union publishes
Consumer Reports, a consumer
information magazine. They
also have a used car price guide,
available by telephone:
(900) 466-0500, $1.75 per
minute, average calls
lasting 5 minutes or more.

▸ **Credco (First
American Credco)
9444 Balboa Ave.,
Ste. 500
San Diego, CA
92123
800-637-2422 -
general
800-255-0792 -
sales department
information**

Credco offers the First
American Instant Merge
Report, a comprehensive
credit report combining
the credit reports from
the Big 3 - TRW, Equifax,
and Trans Union. The
Instant Merge Report takes
three weeks to receive and
costs $28.95.

▸ **Credit Union
National
A s s o c i a t i o n
(CUNA)
5710 Mineral Point
Road**

Madison, WI
53705
608-231-4000

CUNA can help you locate a credit union in your area or help you with questions or problems relating to credit unions.

▸ **Debtors Anonymous**
P.O. Box 400,
Grand Central Station
New York, NY
10163-0400
212-642-8220

Debtors Anonymous is an organization of self-help groups, based on Alcoholics Anonymous, whose purpose of to help people who have chronic and hard-to-handle problems with recurring debt. The telephone number above will allow you to leave your name and address to receive information on the group.

▸ **Department of**
Consumer and

Regulatory Affairs
614 H St. NW
Washington, DC
20001
202-727-7170

▸ **Department of**
Justice
10th &
Constitution
Avenue, NW
Washington, DC
20530
202-514-2000

The Department of Justice can help with a l l types of complaints against creditors.

▸ **Diners Club**
P.O. Box 6003
The Lakes, NV
80901
800-234-6377

▸ **Discover Card**
2500 Lakecook
Road
Riverwood, IL
60015
800-347-2683

▸ **Equifax Information Service Center**
P.O. Box 105873
Atlanta, GA 30348
800-685-1111 -
24-hour
voice mail system
Fax: 404-612-2668

Reports are $8.00, first report free for consumers living in Maryland, and each additional report is $5.00. First report free for consumers living in Vermont, each additional report is $7.50. Reports are $3.00 in Maine.

One free report if credit or other benefits have been denied within the past 60 days.

▸ **Federal**
Communication
Commission (FCC)
Mass Media Bureau
1919 M Street, NW
Washington, DC
20554
202-418-2600

Complain to the FCC of you have been the victim of a fraudulent mass media advertising campaign.

▸ **Federal Deposit**
I n s u r a n c e
Corporation
Office of
Consumer
Programs
550 Seventeenth
St. N.W.
Washington, D.C.
20429

For questions about non-member federally insured banks.

▸ **F e d e r a l**
I n f o r m a t i o n
Center
P.O. Box 1600
Cumberland, MD
21501-1600
301-722-9098

They can help you locate a government agency or give you information on government services.

Federal Information Centers for the Individual States: 800-688-9889 or 800-347-1997

▶ **Federal Trade Commission 6th and Pennsylvania Ave. NW Washington, DC 20580 202-326-2222**

Regional offices:

1718 Peachtree St. NW
Atlanta, GA 30367
404-347-4836

101 Merrimac St., Ste. 810
Boston, MA 02114-4719
617-424-5960

55 East Monroe St..
Ste. 1437
Chicago, IL 60603

312-353-4423

668 Euclid Ave.,
Ste. 520-A
Cleveland, OH 44114
216-522-4207

100 N. Central Expressway, Ste. 500
Dallas, TX 75201
214-767-5501

1961 Stout St., Ste. 1523
Denver, CO 80294
303-844-2271

1100 Wilshire Blvd.,
Suite 13209
Los Angeles, CA 90024
310-235-7890/7595

150 William Street,
Ste 1300
New York, NY 10038
212-264-1207

901 Market St., Ste.
570
San Francisco, CA
94103
415-744-7920

2806 Federal Bldg.,
915 Second Ave.
Seattle, WA 98174
206-220-6363

▶ **Federal Trade
Commission
Public Reference
Washington, DC
20580
202-326-2222**

Free brochures and publications
on credit, including transcripts
of laws pertaining to credit.

▶ **Government Printing
Office
Superintendent of
Documents
P.O. Box 371954
Pittsburgh, PA
15250-7954
202-512-1800
FAX: 202-
512-2250**

The GPO offers "Consumer
Publications," a catalog of
documents   published by
the federal government.

▶ **MasterCard
International, Inc.
12115 Lackland
Rd.
St.   Louis,   MO
63146
314-275-6100**

▶ **Medical
Information
Bureau (MIB)
Box 105
Boston, MA 02112
617-426-3660**

The Medical Information
Bureau stores information
on consumers' medical
conditions and history,
driving records, credit
records, criminal records,
etc. Reports are available
for $8 per copy.

▶ **National   Credit
Union**

**Administration
1776 G St. N.W.
Washington, D.C.
20456**

For questions about federal credit unions.

▸ **Office of Thrift
Supervision
Consumer Affairs
Program
1700 G St. N.W.
Washington, D.C.
20552**

For questions about federally insured savings and loans and federally chartered state banks.

▸ **RAM Research
Cardtrak
P.O. Box 1700
Frederick, MD 21702
800-344-7714**

Cardtrak is a credit periodical listing hundreds of Visa and MasterCards, low interest rate, gold and secured cards. Call the telephone

number above for information on ordering.

**Trans Union
Consumer
Relations
P.O. Box 390
Springfield, PA
19064-0390
216- 779-7200 -
24 hour voice-mail
system**

Reports are mailed within 72 hours. Reports are $8.00 for an individual and $16.00 for a joint report for you and your spouse. One report free if credit, employment or insurance have been denied within the past 60 days. If requesting a credit report after having been denied credit, call: (601) 933-1200

▸ **TRW Consumer
Information
Service
P.O. Box 2104
Allen, TX 75002**

**800-392-1122 -
English and Spanish
24 hour voice mail
system.**

If you live in Maine,   the
report is $2.00, in Maryland,
$5.00, and in   Vermont, $7.50.
One report free if credit,
employment   or insurance
have   been denied within
the past 30 days.   One report
free per year, and each
additional report   is
$8.00.

► **U.   S.   General
Accounting   Office
P.O. Box 6015
Gaithersburg, MD
20877
202-512-6000**

The U.S.G.A. offers   free
publications on credit.

► **Visa International
P.O. Box 8999
San Francisco, CA
94128
415-570-3200**

Glossary

- A -

Account - record of debit and credit transactions covering a certain period of time; an agreement between a creditor and a debtor

Account History - a record of debits and payments for a given account over a certain period of time

Accrue - to accumulate or be added periodically

Affinity Card - a credit card issued by a major credit card company through a smaller company, i.e., a credit union, bearing the logos of both companies

Alternative Credit File - a new credit file set up by someone to avoid the use of the original credit file because of a bad credit history; it is against the law

Amortization - the gradual reduction of a debt (including mortgages) by payment of a loan

Annual fee - a set charge for the use of a credit card each year

Annual percentage rate - what credit costs per year, expressed as a percentage

Application fee - a charge for applying for a credit card

Arbitration - the submission of a dispute to a neutral party (i.e., a judge) for settlement

Assets - property which can be used to pay debts

Associated Subscribers - companies which pay a fee to credit card companies in order to be able to access an individual's credit record

Available Balance - the amount of credit remaining in a credit card account

-B-

Balance - the amount of debt remaining in a credit card account

Bank Account - an amount of money on deposit with a bank

Bankruptcy - a state of insolvency which results in a person being declared by law as subject to having his the benefit of financial affairs administered under the bankruptcy laws for his creditors

Billing Date - the exact date that a bill was issued by the credit card company

Billing Error - a mistake in a credit card bill

Budget - a plan for income and expenditures for a certain period of time

Business Loan - an amount of money given for a certain period of time for the purposes of starting or enhancing a business

-C-

Capacity - one of the "Four C's" of credit scoring; a determination of one's ability to repay a loan

Capital - possessions which can be used to bring in income

Capital Gain - profit from the increase in value of capital

Capital Loss - money lost from the decrease in value of capital

Cardholder - the person responsible for a credit card account

Cardholder Agreement - the written conditions of a credit card account

Carrying Charges - a charge added to the price of merchandise bought on the installment plan

Cash Advance - money borrowed in the form of cash from a credit card account

Chapter 7 - a form of bankruptcy in which all assets are liquidated to pay debts

Chapter 11 - a form of bankruptcy which allows businesses to continue operating while satisfying their debts

Chapter 12 - a form of bankruptcy specifically designed to permit farmers to keep their farms while paying off their debts

Chapter 13 - a form of bankruptcy in which sets up a repayment plan out of present and future income

Character - one of the "Four C's" of credit scoring; a determination of a person's willingness to pay their debts

Charge Account - credit issued by a retail store

Charge Card - the card used to activate a credit account

Chargeoff - a debt that a creditor considers as non-collectible

Closed Account - a credit account which is no longer available to the consumer

Collateral - property or other assets pledged by the borrower to protect the interests of the lender; one of the "Four C's" of credit scoring

Conditions - one of the "Four C's" of credit scoring; economic changes which might affect one's ability to repay a loan

Consolidation - combining several different credit accounts into one account for the purpose of lowering the interest rate and simplifying payment

Consumer Credit Counseling Service - a non-profit organization which helps people settle their debts and organize their finances

Consumer Debt - money owed by a consumer to a creditor

Contract - a legal agreement between two or more parties

Cosigner - one who shares the responsibility for repayment of a loan

Credit - an amount of money placed at a person's disposal, to be paid back at a specified later date

Credit Application - a group of written questions which will be used to determine whether or not you will be extended credit

Credit Bureau - a company that keeps track of consumer credit history, in the form of credit reports

Credit Limit - the dollar amount of credit which a credit company places at the disposal of the consumer

Credit Rating - an estimation of one's ability and willingness to repay a loan, determined by a point system set up by the creditor

Credit Repair - the process of removing negative or erroneous information from one's credit file

Credit Repair Service - a business which charges a fee for helping consumers repair their credit report; this service can be done better, and free of charge, by the consumer himself

Credit Report - a written history of a consumer's credit transactions, kept by credit bureaus

Credit Score - the total amount of points given to a

consumer based on the credit scoring system

Credit Scoring System - a series of criteria set up by a creditor to determine a consumer's ability and willingness to repay a loan

Creditor - one to who a debt is owed

Creditworthiness - the estimation of the amount of risk involved in extending credit to a person

-D-

Debit - a charge against a bank account or a credit card account

Debt- to-Income Ratio - a statement of the percentage of a person's income going to pay debts

Debtor - one who owes money to a creditor

Debit Card - a card issued by a major credit card company in

conjunction with the consumer's bank, which allows point of sale transactions with any merchant honoring the credit card. The funds used to pay for the transaction come directly from the consumer's bank account, not from credit.

Default - failure to pay debts

Delinquent - payments which are overdue

Department Store Account - a charge account with a department store

Disclosure - a statement containing specific information required by law about a credit card account.

Due Date - the date by which payment must be received

-E-

Equal Credit Opportunity Act - a law enacted to prohibit discrimination against credit applicants

Eviction - legally forcing someone to vacate property

-F-

Fair Credit and Charge Card Disclosure Act - a law requiring any company offering credit to state in writing the terms and requirements of the credit

Fair Credit Billing Act - a law designed to protect the consumer from unauthorized charges and errors on the credit card billing statement

Fair Credit Reporting Act - a law which protects the consumer's rights regarding the credit report.

Fair Debt Collection Practices Act - a law governing what a creditor may and may not do in order to collect from a debtor

Federal Trade Commission - an agency of the federal government which regulates the credit industry

Fee - a sum charged for a service

Finance Charges - the total amount of money the consumer pays for using credit - interest charges, service charges, annual fees, and any other fees charges by the credit card company

Foreclosure - attachment of collateral if a debt is not paid

Fraud - intentional deceit in order to induce someone to part with money

-G-

Gold Card - a type of credit card with a large line of credit and special benefits; more

Grace Period - a designated period of time during which the consumer may pay his credit card bill and avoid any finance charges

Gross Pay - the amount of money someone receives in pay before taxes and other deductions are taken

Guarantor - someone who guarantees to pay a debt for someone else

-I-

Index - a point of reference used to determine a change in interest rates

Individual Account - a charge account held by one person who is responsible for any charges

Inquiries - notations on the credit report of consumers who request credit from a company or institution

Installment Credit - a credit account which requires payments of a specific amount to be paid at specific intervals until the loan is paid

Interest Charge - money charged for interest payments on a credit card account

Interest Rate - a percentage charged for an amount of money borrowed

-J-

Joint Account - a credit account held by more than one person, with all parties being equally responsible for the debt

Judgment - a legal decision handed down by a court

-L-

Late Charges - a fee assessed for not paying a debt by the agreed- upon time

Late Payments - a payment not made by the agreed-upon date

Liability - legal obligation to pay a debt

Lien - a legal claim on property for the satisfaction of a debt. Property may not be sold until all liens on that property are satisfied.

Loan - money lent at interest

-M-

Minimum Payment - the smallest amount of money that will be accepted as payment for a credit card account

Mortgage - a legal promise securing real property in payment for debt

-N-

Negative Information - entries on a credit report which are to the disadvantage of the consumer

Net Pay - the amount of money received in salary after taxes and other predetermined deductions are taken

-O-

Open Account - a credit account which requires payment within 30, 60, or 90 days (e.g., American Express)

Open-Ended Credit - a credit account that may be used over and over again; revolving credit

Outstanding Balance - the amount owed on a credit account at any given time

Over-the-Limit - the amount of charges exceeding the line of credit on a credit account

Outdated Information - any information on the credit report which is no longer valid

-P-

Payment - a certain amount of money given to a creditor, usually monthly, to satisfy a debt

Personal Information - details about the consumer's finances and lifestyle used to determine the credit score

Personal Identification Number (PIN) - a number known only to the consumer which may be used to activate a credit account at an Automatic Teller Machine

Personal Loan - an amount of cash lent to an individual

Personal Property - items owned by a consumer which are not considered real property (automobiles, jewelry, etc.)

Point-of-Sale - the place where an item is bought; this term is used to apply to purchases made with a debit card, as opposed to a credit card

Points - a specific charge by a lender for a loan. Normally each point equals one percent of the loan and is paid up front.

-R-

Real Property - fixed or immovable property, e.g., land or a home

Rebate - the return of a part of a payment

Rebate Card - a credit card offering specific rebates on purchases made using the card

Revolving Credit - a credit account which may be used

repeatedly until a specified limit is reached, and that requires regular payments

-S-

Secured Credit Card - a credit account which requires a deposit to be made with the bank, which is used as collateral against the line of credit

Service Charge - a fee assessed by the credit company for services rendered

Small Business Administration - a non-profit group which helps small business with low- interest loans and free business counseling

Small Claims Court - a state court which handles legal disputes involving small amounts of money (usually around $5,000) with very low legal fees

-T-

Tiered Rate - an interest rate which becomes lower as the customer's outstanding balance increases

Transaction Fee - a fee charged for each credit card transaction

Truth in Lending Act - a law which requires creditors to reveal in writing specific information about the cost of buying on credit or taking out a loan

-U-

Unsecured card - a credit card which does not require a deposit to be held in collateral with the bank; a regular credit card

-V-

Variable Rate - an interest rate that is tied to an index ; a changing interest rate, such as the prime rate

Index

- D -

- E -

- F -

- G -

- I -

- U -

- V -

- W -